Online Safety
for Children and Teens
on the Autism Spectrum

of related interest

Cyberbullying
Activities to Help Children and Teens to Stay Safe in a
Texting, Twittering, Social Networking World
Vanessa Rogers
ISBN 978 1 84905 105 7
eISBN 978 0 85700 228 0

Asperger Syndrome and Bullying
Strategies and Solutions
Nick Dubin
Foreword by Michael John Carley
ISBN 978 1 84310 846 7
eISBN 978 1 84642 635 3

Parenting without Panic
A Pocket Support Group for Parents of Children and Teens
on the Autism Spectrum (Asperger's Syndrome)
Brenda Dater
ISBN 978 1 84905 941 1
eISBN 978 0 85700 958 6

Parenting ASD Teens
A Guide to Making it Up As You Go
Andrew Schlegelmilch
ISBN 978 1 84905 975 6
eISBN 978 0 85700 921 0

The Aspie Girl's Guide to Being Safe with Men
The Unwritten Safety Rules No-one is Telling You
Debi Brown
Foreword by Sarah Attwood
ISBN 978 1 84905 354 9
eISBN 978 0 85700 703 2

The Autism Spectrum, Sexuality and the Law
What every parent and professional needs to know
Tony Attwood, Isabelle Hénault and Nick Dubin
ISBN 978 1 84905 919 0
eISBN 978 0 85700 679 0

Online Safety
for Children and Teens
on the Autism Spectrum

A Parent's and Carer's Guide

NICOLA LONIE

Jessica Kingsley *Publishers*
London and Philadelphia

First published in 2015
by Jessica Kingsley Publishers
73 Collier Street
London N1 9BE, UK
and
400 Market Street, Suite 400
Philadelphia, PA 19106, USA

www.jkp.com

Library of Congress Cataloging in Publication Data
A CIP catalog record for this book is available from the Library of Congress

British Library Cataloguing in Publication Data
A CIP catalogue record for this book is available from the British Library

ISBN 978 1 84905 454 6
eISBN 978 0 85700 870 1

Printed and bound in Great Britain by Bell & Bain Ltd, Glasgow

This book is dedicated to my two
beautiful children, Liam and Molly-Mae.

Acknowledgements

I would like to take this opportunity to acknowledge the help and support I received both professionally and personally from the staff and trustees of Autism Concern, without whose dedication and commitment many children in Northamptonshire with autism would have little or no support. I am very pleased to be able to donate a percentage of the proceeds from this publication to Autism Concern.[1]

A very special thank you goes to Julia Hardcastle. A mentor and friend indeed!

For my special friend Dan, thank you for your patience – and for your valuable input. I could not have completed this project without your much-appreciated time, love and support.

Thanks also to my Mum and stepfather John Thomson, who did their best to ensure I had a good education as a child. I can never repay them for that, but I hope a copy of this book and a big thank you is a start.

Some of the artwork in this book was created by Ellen Lynn Bryson Davis – a talented artist in Northamptonshire.[2]

I would also like to thank Emily McClave of Jessica Kingsley Publishers for her encouragement and help during the writing of this book.

1   For more information see www.autismconcern.org.
2   See www.etsy.com/shop/eldartashealing.

Contents

Preface

While working on this book I saw a funny and insightful slogan online, 'The good thing about being over 40 is that we did most of our stupid sh*t before the internet.' This slogan applies to me – I am in my late forties – and it made me laugh. I was in my twenties before having real access or 'alone time' with a computer and this was only at work, and even then they didn't do that much apart from be able to correct, print and save word processing documents – no internet or web back then – but they fascinated me! A home computer was a bit out of my price range in the early days, but I did experiment with the early Amstrads and Amigas, both with gaming and programming.

Computer enthusiasts will understand when I say that the first time I had a home computer connected to the internet was one of the most exciting days in my life – even though it was a frustratingly slow dial-up system (others, of course, will think I am crazy). Television as a general form of entertainment, for me, instantly took second place. I had the world in my hands from the comfort of my own home; why would I want to watch so much television now that I had this amazing source of information and interaction possibilities, or when would I even have the time?

When my son was five years old we had just moved with my husband's job from Aberdeen to Northamptonshire.

We had always suspected there was 'something not quite right' with our son, but the doctors didn't seem to understand and it was difficult to explain to them exactly what was wrong. Yes, my son was healthy, but he seemed so different, so distant and unaware of others around him.

My son's first junior school was in Northamptonshire and I will never forget his first half-day, as he dressed in his neat school uniform. What a lovely morning that was – until I went to pick him up and the school took me aside and said that they were sorry but they 'just couldn't provide for his needs' and I was to contact the education department of the local council. They were very helpful and I did understand that it was not their fault that Liam was too difficult for them to cope with and look after properly – there was a big class of other deserving students, all demanding the teacher's attention.

Eventually my son was diagnosed a year or so later and was 'statemented', enabling him to access special educational needs facilities.

After the diagnosis, the paediatrician recommended we visit Autism Concern for more information as we were baffled as to what exactly autism was and what it meant for us as a family. I had a vague recollection of Dustin Hoffman in the movie *Rain Man* being autistic, but that was as far as my knowledge of the subject went. I actually remember saying to the doctor, 'Like *Rain Man*?'

I can never begin to explain how grateful I am for the support and kindness I received from the staff and trustees at Autism Concern. They were so helpful in so many ways, right from our first relaxing, informative and enjoyable meeting, and without their help my son and I would not be so happy and content in our lives today – of that I am absolutely sure.

I had just completed a web design course and offered Autism Concern my services on a voluntary basis to update their website. This quickly opened up to the offer of part-time employment, which I gladly accepted. I worked for Autism Concern as their IT specialist and webmaster for approximately 11 years (2001–12).

One of the most incredible women I have ever met is Julia Hardcastle, the Managing Director of Autism Concern. Her dedication and commitment to improving the lives of those touched by autism in Northamptonshire is amazing and I owe so much of my knowledge to her.

In 2010, Autism Concern received a grant and I was asked to design and create internet safety courses for children with special educational needs (SEN) in various schools throughout Northamptonshire. I worked very closely with autism experts and experienced teaching staff and the project was extremely successful and beneficial for the child with SEN.

It was because of this, which was an incredible experience and a massive learning curve for me, and the interest around autism and computers, that I decided I should write a book to help families with autistic children safely use a computer and the internet.

The internet, in my humble opinion, is an amazing piece of modern technology – you can easily find information on *any* subject without even having to leave the comfort of your own home. I am still excited each time I open up my browser. However, at the same time, I am glad I am not a child in this day and age, exposed to all the potential threats children face constantly while online.

I believe that the internet can be an extremely positive learning tool for all children – and *especially* for those children with high-functioning autism who have natural talents with computers – but *only* if it is used with precaution, supervision, safety and guidance.

I hope the strategies I have included in this book prove to be useful – they helped me!

CHAPTER 1

Autism and Computers

The Pros and Cons

INTRODUCTION

Autism is a life-long developmental disability that affects both social and communication skills and is thought to have neurological and/or genetic causes. These causes are not yet fully understood and there is no known cure. *The skills most likely to be affected in people with autism include communication and social interaction, and they have difficulty with flexibility of thought, imagination and play.* This is often referred to as The Triad of Impairments, and attributed to Lorna Wing and Judith Gould (Wing and Gould 1979).

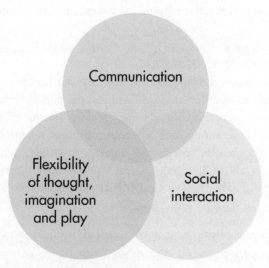

Figure 1.1 The Triad of Impairments
(adapted from Lorna Wing and Judith Gould)

Autistic people can also often exhibit features such as a restricted range of interests and repetitive actions. More often than not, a person with autism has difficulties in these three main areas of their development, but other skills may develop typically.

AUTISM AND COMPUTERS: THE PROS

Some high-functioning autistic children (and adults) can have exceptional skills and aptitude in computer use, and their abilities with computers and technology can be amazing.

Many autistic children have the ability to understand computers better than they understand other people, and some experts believe this is because the autistic mind processes information *visually* – as does a computer. The brain of a child with autism stores memories and knowledge in a photo-type format, that is, each memory is stored visually in the mind. This is similar to how a computer works – a logical and ordered visual processing system.

This remarkable ability should always be encouraged and supported, but parents and carers of autistic children need to be fully aware of the potential risks that face their child while online, know what to do if anything goes wrong, and be ready to take action.

Due to the recent advances in technology, parents/carers and teachers of autistic children now have an abundance of new and innovative tools to help them help the child in their care, such as hardware (i.e. touch-screen monitors), software programs, websites and applications.

Computers can help your autistic child develop different skills
COMMUNICATION AND SOCIAL SKILLS

The causes of speech and language difficulties in autism are still unknown. Some experts believe that these difficulties are caused by a variety of conditions that occur before, during, or after birth, affecting brain development, but as yet nothing has been confirmed scientifically.

The development of speech and language in children on the autism spectrum often takes a divergent route to that of a neurotypical child, and the autistic child may display or experience symptoms such as:

- being non-verbal – not speaking
- speaking, but using language in unusual or uncommon ways
- speaking only single words
- repeating a mimicked phrase over and over

- repeating what they hear (a condition called echolalia)
- being unable to imagine another person's state of mind or point of view
- having a restricted capacity to symbolise, e.g. unable to understand body language
- lacking eye contact
- lacking attention
- being unable to point out objects
- not understanding the 'give and take' during conversations.

Some autistic children have sensory problems or can be oversensitive and this means that they may in fact find the feeling of their own tongue, teeth and/or lips touching each other to be so disagreeable or unpleasant that they simply avoid talking.

Please remember that the inability to communicate successfully with others *does not mean* that people with autism are unintelligent or unaware.

Autistic children can often find computers and the internet extremely valuable instruments to help them with communication difficulties. Some autistic children, in fact, may prefer to interact with a computer rather than other people directly because the technology can be less intimidating and/or stressful than face-to-face conversations, and a computer may provide a more motivating medium.

Typically, children with autism have difficulties/barriers with their communication and social skills in one way or other, and friends/family and peers can seem unapproachable because of this.

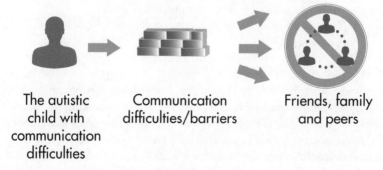

The autistic child with communication difficulties

Communication difficulties/barriers

Friends, family and peers

Figure 1.2 Communication difficulties/barriers

However, with the aid of a computer and the internet, friends, family and peers can communicate with the autistic child via a stress-free and undemanding environment, with no need for direct touch or even eye contact. The computer simplifies the amount of information needed for the child to communicate – and therefore makes communication easier and less challenging for the child.

| The autistic child with communication difficulties | Communication stress free/ undemanding | Friends, family and peers |

Figure 1.3 Using computers to communicate

REAL-LIFE STORY – ROBERT

Robert is a non-verbal autistic teenager who has severe problems communicating with others. However, he is very computer literate and has enjoyed playing technology-based role-playing games for many years on both his computer and gamestation, and this is his principal hobby.

Robert's parents, however, were concerned with their son's lack of interaction with others and decided to try to use his love of games and computer ability to enhance his communication skills.

With his parents' help and supervision, Robert discovered that he could 'talk' (using text typing) to other players via the game software and with a connection to the internet. Robert was naturally very cautious at first, unwilling to learn how to control the settings for this option of the game, but gradually he began to understand the advantages of 'talking' to others about his passion. He soon took charge, quickly gaining confidence and enjoying a new-found audience of like-minded individuals whom he could converse with on his terms and without face-to-face confrontation or the need for speech.

Not only has Robert made 'friends' online, he is now a regular and popular reviewer of games on a large website. His opinions on games are held in high esteem by the online gaming community.

The best news is that Robert, with encouragement and support from his parents and those around him, is now attending college on a part-time basis, working towards a BSc (Hons) in Computer Games Development. His parents and the college professionals who work closely with Robert have high hopes that he will secure a job designing and developing game software in the future.

UNDERSTANDING OF BODY LANGUAGE

The body language of children with autism can be difficult for many of us to understand. Facial expressions, movements and gestures may be easily misunderstood and misinterpreted, and may seem threatening.

Most of us are unaccustomed to autistic body language, and because in a lot of instances their language may not be speech, autistic children do struggle to let others know what they want or need. As any of us may do in such a situation, the autistic child may scream in frustration or resort to grabbing, or even pushing, when they want something and cannot communicate this need easily to others.

On the reverse side, children with autism do not typically understand *your* body language. They often need additional help and teaching to identify properly body language such as facial expressions and hand movements.

Figure 1.4 Using a computer to understand body language

With computers, and specific software now widely available online, parents and carers can help their autistic child develop an understanding of body language and can teach the child new skills such as facial recognition using colourful, easy-to-use interactive technology.

REAL-LIFE STORY – SAM

Sam is an autistic child who does not understand other people's body language. Using a camera connected to a computer, Sam's mother Jane took clear photographs of her face wearing various expressions. She then used a photo-editing software program to type in the descriptive word for each expression in bold lettering just under her face in the photograph.

Jane then printed out the expression photographs onto small easy-to-use cards and she used these when teaching Sam about body language.

Jane was patient and it was a slow start, but because Sam was familiar with his mother's face and in a relaxed environment, he began to recognise the different expressions worn by her in the photos.

Sam was eventually able to carry this new skill on into the real world and began to identify facial expressions in others too. It was noted by his school that there was a great improvement of facial expression recognition when Sam interacted with other boys in his class and with his teachers.

PLANNING AND ORGANISING SKILLS

Autistic children usually do better when they have a highly structured schedule or routine set up and most parents/carers will already utilise this method to help their child. Most parents/carers know to set up a schedule for their child with regular times for meals, school and bedtime, for example, and to attempt to keep disruptions to this routine to a minimum.

If you have not yet done this for your autistic child, it is highly recommended that you do so. You can do this more quickly and effectively using a computer. There are now many advanced software options available which will aid the creation of schedules for your autistic child. It is a good idea to research these software programs thoroughly before purchase in order to find the most suitable one for your own computer literacy levels as well as your child's requirements.

Autistic children find planning, organising and prioritising very challenging and some may have difficulty with 'cognitive function' – the intellectual process by which we think, remember, reason and understand ideas.

Many of us use certain strategies, techniques and tools to help us organise our day and prioritise tasks; for example, we might make a shopping list or write birthdays on a calendar. These strategies can also be very effective for autistic children, especially if they're used regularly and consistently by all those who support them.

One benefit of computers and other technology such as mobile phones is that they can be used to store important information, instructions, schedules and/or reminders for your autistic child.

REAL-LIFE STORY – SARAH

Sarah is a high-functioning young autistic woman in her late teens who struggles to remember when to do certain tasks such as go to bed, bathe and attend her further education course. She also works part time in a large chemist and therefore needs to be fully organised in order to succeed in her busy life.

Sarah and her parents use both her computer and her mobile telephone to keep accurate up-to-date schedules, records and diaries.

Sarah's schedule and daily appointments are printed from the computer each morning. The day's timetable is also sent to her mobile phone in the form of a simple-to-access and easy-to-read text document in case she loses the hard copy. Sarah's parents will text her with reminders of important appointments.

Sarah can now confidently go about her busy day using this consistent reminder facility when needed.

WRITING AND RECORDING SKILLS

Some autistic children can actually find word processing on the computer easier than recording by hand, as many struggle with handwriting due to poor motor skills. For some autistic children, the keyboard is easier to use than a pen or pencil. Word processors can also offer a safe and controllable environment in which the child can play, experiment, explore and be creative, with the opportunity to undo mistakes easily and/or to try again.

The computer is beneficial to the autistic child because it can also be set to automate many tasks, helping the child to complete certain tasks quickly and easily. This can be useful when the child is disorganised or has poor motor skills or is obsessed by attention to detail.

Giving an autistic child a starting point can also be very useful – this could simply be a list of words with key subjects or phrases. For some autistic children, a sequence of pictures or symbols may be helpful to encourage writing.

Also, a well-ordered and neat printed page will be far more pleasing to your child than a poorly handwritten piece of work.

For those autistic children experiencing difficulties with reading or spelling, speech feedback software (i.e. the computer 'reads aloud' what is on the screen) can be effective, and the spell-check option available in most word processing software packages can help motivate the self-checking of work.

If your child does not have particular strengths with the mouse and/ or keyboard, consider using a touch-screen monitor to support writing.

REAL-LIFE STORY – MARY

Mary is a high-functioning autistic teenager who, although she attends mainstream school, has difficulties with fine motor skills. Her handwriting has always been very poor and barely legible and this has caused problems for her teachers and with her school work, as well as being extremely frustrating for Mary. With agreement from her school, Mary was allowed to produce all her work using a laptop with word processing software installed.

The results were immediate. Instantly, Mary found that she was less stressed about doing her school work, and her grades improved significantly.

Her parents and teachers were simply amazed by the overall improvement.

ATTENTION SPAN/FOCUS

Most of us have 'polytrophic interest systems'. This means that we are capable of multiple divided attention spans and can usually have many interests active at the same time, while being ready to receive yet more information.

Many children on the autism spectrum also have a condition known as 'monotropism'. This means they have very focused attention to detail and have a restricted capability to keep a range of interests active at the same time.

Computers can help with this difficulty because the technology can aid the user in combining various focuses of attention effectively, therefore potentially helping them in other areas too.

REAL-LIFE STORY – LUKE

Luke is a non-verbal 14-year-old boy on the autism spectrum. He has a fascination with trains. He enjoys using his computer and the internet to look at photos of trains and maps and he relaxes by memorising timetables. He is a member of a train-spotting website, communicates with other enthusiasts via this method and has made some friends who share his passion.

Before Luke could use a computer and the internet he would insist on daily trips to the train station, which were very difficult to organise and extremely stressful for both him and his carer. Luke is now taken only once a fortnight to the local train station and this is sufficient for his needs, allowing his carer time to concentrate more on Luke's other requirements.

Luke has learned to use the computer to combine various focuses successfully and he is also learning to adapt this theory for day-to-day life.

COGNITIVE SKILLS

Computer technology can help some children develop an understanding of cause and effect. There are straightforward software programs available that encourage your child to interact with a simple input device such as a mouse or touch-screen monitor, and this interaction is rewarded by something interesting happening. Usually this software is designed to develop into more complicated interactions suitable for the child's increasing ability and age, and the rewards change to aid motivation.

If your child struggles with a keyboard or mouse there are a number of hardware and software solutions available to overcome these difficulties. For example, consider using a touch-screen monitor, or a concept keyboard – these can reduce the number of keys found on a standard keyboard.

REAL-LIFE STORY – BARRY

Barry is a 17-year-old autistic boy who does not readily interact with others or computers and technology in general. His parents purchased a computer with a large robust touch-screen monitor and initially installed a very basic software game designed to help children develop cognitive skills. Barry has a fascination for dinosaurs and the game incorporates these animals throughout.

Although it took many weeks, eventually Barry, his attention grabbed by the dinosaurs, began to enjoy the fact that when he pressed the correct section of the screen at the correct time, he was rewarded by the roar of a dinosaur.

His parents have now introduced new games incorporating other animals and characters, and Barry's cognitive skills are steadily improving.

HAND–EYE CO-ORDINATION SKILLS

Hand–eye co-ordination is the processing of information visually to guide hand movements. We need good hand–eye co-ordination for a variety of everyday activities, from picking up an apple to using the television remote control.

Unfortunately, poor hand–eye co-ordination often goes with autism spectrum disorders. It is a commonly accepted fact nowadays, confirmed by numerous studies, that playing computer or video games can improve hand–eye co-ordination as this helps to develop the ability to work both hands and eyes together simultaneously.

Because the game player has to use an external device, such as a controller or mouse, to control the game, their brain has constantly to be thinking about performing the real-world commands, such as clicking the mouse, that will in turn be performing the desired actions in the game. Even using simple key-pressing games such as *Tetris*, your child's brain still needs to convert what it wants to achieve into what button to press. This helps to exercise hand–eye co-ordination.

REAL-LIFE STORY – SALLY

Sally has struggled with hand–eye co-ordination difficulties since infancy, the most frustrating part of this being that she could not easily tie up her shoelaces, taking up to an hour if left unaided.

When she was seven years old, Sally's parents introduced her to a simple game installed on the home computer which was designed specifically to help improve hand–eye co-ordination problems in children.

The game displayed a variety of large shoes and it was up to the player, in this case Sally, to utilise the mouse correctly in order to tie up the shoelaces. When successful, Sally was rewarded with a cute cartoon character singing her praises and telling her how well she had done.

Sally can now tie up her shoelaces much faster and is very proud of this achievement and ability. She continues to enjoy this 'game' regularly.

MEMORY SKILLS

Remembering requires the ability to store information and is typically divided into three main classifications:

- *Short-term memory.* This is the ability to store information for a few seconds.

- *Active working memory.* This is the ability to store information for several minutes while manipulating the information.

- *Long-term memory.* This is the ability to store information for an extended period of time.

Many autistic children have difficulties with memory, and a popular way for getting their brain cells working is for them to solve puzzles or riddles, which make them think in unusual and/or creative ways.

There is now an abundance of free games on the internet that can be used to develop your child's memory skills; for example, the 'Simon Says' sequence game, where players have to try to remember a sequence of colours in the correct order.

Remember, the more children exercise their memory muscle, the easier it will be for them to recognise, remember and process information.

REAL-LIFE STORY – LIAM

Liam is a high-functioning autistic teenager who attends mainstream school. He has many issues and really struggles with memory problems. He became extremely stressed and distraught when informed that he would be required to memorise lines for his small role in the school play.

Rather than simply allow their son to avoid his role in the play, and in order to help him with this particular difficulty, Liam's parents input his lines into a word processing document in a large decorative font and broke each line down into very small portions.

Liam's parents then printed these small 'chunks' onto card and used this to help their son learn his lines by turning it into a game.

Liam's memory of the lines improved so much that he is looking forward to his bigger role in the school play next year.

SPATIAL VISUALISATION ABILITY SKILLS

Spatial skills involve the ability to understand problems involving physical spaces, shapes or forms, and the ability mentally to manipulate an object in two or three dimensions.

Spatial ability is the capacity to think about objects and to draw conclusions about those objects from limited information. For example, someone with good spatial abilities might be good at thinking about how an object will look when rotated. These skills are valuable in many real-world situations.

Children on the autism spectrum often have difficulties and display poor performance on tasks requiring good spatial visualisation ability.

However, this ability can be improved with the use of technology and with practice.

REAL-LIFE STORY – STEPHEN

Stephen is a 12-year-old autistic boy with spatial visualisation difficulties. This was apparent from an early age when he failed to finish jigsaw puzzles and would often attempt to connect a piece of the puzzle with a tab on it to another piece with a tab or even to a flat side.

Using computers and the internet, Stephen was encouraged by his parents to play very simple jigsaw puzzle games and gradually his ability to connect the right pieces improved.

Stephen was then able to take this improved skill to the real world and now gets great pleasure playing the jigsaw games his parents and grandparents buy for him from the shops, as well as finding his own to play online.

Computers have also been shown to:

- *alleviate stress in autistic children:* a computer not only thinks visually, like your autistic child, but is also a controllable and unthreatening object which, if used properly, can provide a relaxing environment that helps to relieve or reduce stress
- *be therapeutic for autistic children:* computers are not just educational but can be therapeutic for the autistic child and offer an environment for play/using the imagination, sociability, exploration and creativity.

REAL-LIFE STORY – CALLUM

Callum is a low-functioning autistic child who often shows signs of stress and regularly becomes aggressive. When the family installed a computer at home, and Callum started spending time using the internet, mostly playing crossword-type games, he became calmer and more communicative with his parents.

Although Callum's parents appreciate the benefits the internet has provided for their son, and the way it can help reduce his stress levels, they always ensure that they limit his computer time to discourage overuse or addiction.

How will technology continue to help autistic people in the future?

The future of computer technology is up for debate; who knows where it will lead us? At the moment, studies and research continue into the benefits of computers and technology for autistic children.

The organisation Hacking Autism is pulling together a volunteer group of software developers and leading autism specialists to develop groundbreaking, touch-enabled applications for the autism community and to improve the lives of people with autism.

AUTISM AND COMPUTERS – THE CONS

There are many positive benefits (pros) for the child with autism when safely using computers and the internet, but now we must discuss the dangers and risks (cons), and unfortunately there are many (see Figure 1.5).

It is essential that parents/carers of autistic children are fully aware of *all* the potential dangers.

These dangers are (but not limited to):

- your child being exposed to violent and/or sexually explicit images
- your child being contacted by sexual predators in chat rooms, on social media websites and by email
- your child becoming obsessed with or fixated on games or social networking websites
- depending on their skills, your child being exploited as a hacker – manipulated into creating spyware, viruses or trojans for unscrupulous individuals or organisations to use to their advantage
- cyberbullying and/or harassment
- your child having a debit or credit card (if they are above a certain age) which can be easily exploited if in the wrong hands, or which your child may use to spend excessively online

- your child disclosing personal information, such as their school name or their email address, which makes it easy for predators to track and locate them
- infection of the computer by spyware and viruses: if your child visits unsuitable websites it increases the chance of your computer becoming infected
- excessive commercialism: advertising and product-related websites can bombard your autistic child with unsuitable content and images
- plagiarism and cheating: it can be very easy for your child to copy other people's work and try to pass it off as their own
- health-related illnesses caused by excessive computer use and bad posture.

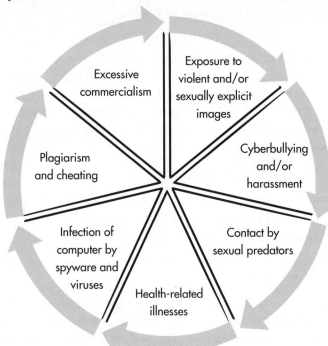

Figure 1.5 The most common risks and dangers your autistic child faces while online

Why are autistic children more at risk?

It is understood that children with SEN (and therefore autistic children) are at greater risk of online dangers, such as cyberbullying, therefore you should be extra careful when allowing your autistic child to use a computer and the internet.

> Vulnerable groups at greater risk include children with special educational needs (SEN).
>
> (Department for Education 2011, p.3)

Because of the nature of autism, the autistic child will not naturally fully understand the potential threats and dangers present when using a computer and the internet, unlike neurotypical children who can often detect when something is a 'lie', 'wrong' or 'not quite right'.

Because of their lack of social skills, social naïvety and/or obsessive compulsive disorders autistic children may not typically be able to determine fact from fiction/opinions, may not understand social cues or internet text/language and may, in general, be very easily manipulated by others, such as paedophiles, or be exploited to use their computer skills and talent and become involved in hacking/cracking.

In the last few years and due to the huge rise in the technology available to autistic children, it has come to light that many 'hackers' are believed to be on the autism spectrum. There have been widely publicised arrests and criminal proceedings against teenagers on the spectrum who have broken laws but who may not have fully understood that what they were doing was wrong. For more information on hacking see Chapter 8, Computer Hacking and Autism.

Many children on the autism spectrum show obsessive, repetitive behaviour as a way to cope with everyday life, and computers and the internet can increase this tendency because the child is typically able to interact with something they deem safe and user friendly and is normally left alone for long periods. For more information on addiction see Chapter 4, Computer/Gaming Addiction and the Autistic Child.

REAL-LIFE STORY – BRUCE

Bruce is a high-functioning autistic teenager who attends mainstream school and enjoys computer programming as his principal hobby.

While learning how to create a specific command in a program, Bruce joined an internet forum for computer programmers and experts and began to chat to other members via the discussion board.

Bruce was contacted by a fellow computer programmer, who had the knowledge to help Bruce solve his computer problem, and because of this Bruce respected this man and an online friendship quickly developed. After a few weeks of frequent online conversations, Bruce agreed to meet up face to face with his new friend – and never even thought to explain to his parents that the friend he was meeting was an online friend and not a real friend.

Unfortunately in this case the outcome was not good. The computer programmer who befriended Bruce turned out to be a paedophile who abused the poor boy extensively over a period of time, before being caught and convicted.

In summary, the risks to the autistic child while using computers and the internet are higher than those for the neurotypical child and therefore it is recommended that their computer use be fully monitored by a responsible and knowledgeable adult at all times.

What can I do to help?

You have taken the first step by purchasing/borrowing this book. The next very important step in order to be able to take part in your child's computer and internet experiences is to educate yourself initially – by continuing to read the rest of this book! This will empower you so that you know what your autistic child is doing and have the knowledge to put a stop to any illegal or unpleasant pursuits and be aware of any threats.

CHAPTER 2

An Introduction to the Internet and Internet Safety

INTRODUCTION

The internet plays a big part in most of our lives today. Ofcom reports:

> Over a million new fixed broadband connections were added in 2012. The total number of fixed broadband connections continued to grow in 2012, increasing by 5.4% year on year to 21.7 million. Ofcom research indicates that 72% of UK homes had a fixed broadband connection.
>
> (Ofcom 2013c)

Although a large majority of children throughout the world are now educated in the classroom on how to utilise and take advantage of the internet and modern technology effectively, past generations of parents and carers may have missed out on this valuable training. This means that parents and carers may be less confident in their computer ability than their young child/teen and therefore feel inadequate to question, control and support their child's online activity.

Even professionals, such as social workers, who support children on the autism spectrum (no matter what their level of computer literacy may be) can gain from reading this book as they too need to know what danger signs to look out for, the potential capabilities and skills of the child in their care and also how to help the child stay safe online.

This book is most suited to parents/carers and professionals who support autistic children/teens and who may have limited computer experience or skills but understand the basics of how to access the internet.

It is the aim of this book to provide all the information needed to help parents and carers to monitor, educate and guide their autistic child/teen's computer and internet use *safely*, including key concerns such as parental control, social networking, grooming, cyberbullying, computer addiction and hacking.

The risks and the warning signs to look out for are also discussed in this book, alongside useful advice and examples from real-life experiences.

The practical solutions in this book, if used correctly, will help give parents and carers peace of mind and ensure that their autistic child can enjoy the full educational and social benefits of the internet in a totally safe environment.

WHAT IS THE INTERNET?

The internet is a global collection of computers that can connect to each other via 'networks' and it was originally created by the US Defense Department's Advanced Research Projects Agency in the 1960s.

Around this time, many other 'networks' were being designed and developed by both government and commercial companies, and in different countries, but the experts struggled to connect the 'networks' successfully to each other.

In 1974, however, Vint Cerf and Bob Kahn developed TCP/IP, 'a Protocol for Packet Network Interconnection' which successfully allowed different networks to connect together – and the internet was born!

WHAT IS THE WORLD WIDE WEB AND IS IT THE SAME AS THE INTERNET?

You could not have the Web (the set of pages that you view using your browser or that you find with search engines such as Google) without the internet. A fun way to describe the difference would be that the internet is the cake and the Web the icing on top. You need the cake to be there before you can put on the icing – but together they are a fantastic recipe for success.

In the late 1980s and early 1990s, researcher Tim Berners-Lee and his team developed the original World Wide Web (also known as the Web).

The Web uses the HTTP Protocol language to transfer data and information back and forth using the internet.

Many people mix up these terms but they are not synonymous.

WHAT IS INTERNET SAFETY?

Do you know what kind of internet safety threats exist and how to protect yourself and your family?

Ask your child *if* and *how* they stay safe online. Do they learn about internet safety at school and if so, do they have any tips for you or can they teach you what they know?

With the growing popularity and accessibility of the internet and the Web, it is only normal that issues such as internet safety are now being raised and openly discussed because it is such an important area for parents/carers to consider these days. Paedophiles, virus threats, hackers, spammers, phishing scams, spyware threats and even cyber-terrorists are just some of the hazards and threats your child faces while online.

The more time you and your family spend online, the more important internet safety should become – it's a subject that should not be ignored or avoided.

> Over 90% of children aged 5–15 have access to, and over 80% of children use, the internet at home.
>
> (Ofcom 2013a)

Internet safety threats can directly cause distress to both adults and children, and some threats can even have life-altering consequences. It is therefore extremely important that you provide your autistic child with a safe and healthy environment, supervision, support and guidance – before, during and after computer use – no matter what age they are!

WHY IS INTERNET SAFETY IMPORTANT?

If *you* don't take internet safety seriously – why should your child?

> 17% of parents are concerned about content on the internet, which is a 6% decrease since 2011.
>
> (Ofcom 2013a)

> 84% of parents agree that 'I trust my child to use the internet safely', which is a 3% increase since 2011.
>
> (Ofcom 2013a)

Internet safety, or internet security as it is sometimes called, is a serious and important issue that needs to be addressed frequently and regularly in order for you to manage and control both present and future security and privacy issues your autistic child may experience when online.

To understand why you need to teach your child about, and encourage, internet safety, it is extremely important that you are aware of the dangers, risks and threats associated with the internet and the Web yourself.

THE MOST COMMON THREATS AND RECOMMENDATIONS

Undesirable network entry or 'hacking'

A person or a software program that can enter your network (and therefore access your computer files and personal information) without your knowledge, approval or permission is one of the major threats as far as internet safety is concerned and should be taken very seriously.

Hacking is when someone 'breaks in' to a network/computer to acquire private information such as passwords, in order to use this information for personal gain or for illegal or offensive purposes. If a hacker gets into your network they could even hack your bank account and steal your money if you bank online.

If you do not have reliable firewall and anti-virus software installed on your child's system they can be extremely vulnerable to these types of attack. It is therefore strongly recommended that you install an anti-virus software program (many are available on the Web to download – some even free of charge for basic packages) or update the version of the one currently running on your system to ensure full protection.

Pornography websites and paedophiles

Unfortunately both the Web and the internet are flooded with pornographic content and sexual predators looking for easy and vulnerable victims to contact and prey on.

Parental control software is highly recommended to block pornographic content and prevent contact from dubious characters.

You should also explain to your autistic child that even if they innocently take and upload a photograph and/or video, they need to be very cautious. Media such as this can be easily altered and misused or even posted on pornographic sites.

Paedophiles typically loiter around the internet and/or Web in the attempt to be friends with and/or groom a child – usually via various 'chat' methods such as instant messaging – and then bully or intimidate that child into meeting in person in order to abuse them.

A large US survey shows that one in 10 children and young people receive sexual solicitations of a distressing or aggressive nature.

(Department for Education 2011, p.3)

Abusers use a range of techniques to make contact and establish relationships with children and young people, including:

- gathering personal details, such as age, name, address, mobile number, name of school and photographs;
- offering opportunities for modelling, particularly to young girls;
- promising meetings with pop idols or celebrities, or offers of merchandise;
- offering cheap tickets to sporting or music events;
- offering material gifts, including electronic games, music or software;
- offering virtual gifts, such as rewards, passwords and gaming cheats;
- suggesting quick and easy ways to make money;
- paying young people to appear naked and perform sexual acts via webcams;
- gaining a child's confidence by offering positive attention and encouraging the child to share or talk about any difficulties or problems at home, and providing a sympathetic and supportive response;

- bullying and intimidating behaviour, such as threatening to expose the child by contacting their parents to inform them of their child's communications or postings on a social networking site, and/or saying they know where the child lives or goes to school;

- using webcams to spy and take photographs and videos of victims;

- asking sexually themed questions, such as 'Do you have a boyfriend?' or 'Are you a virgin?';

- asking children and young people to meet offline;

- sending sexually themed images to a child, depicting adult content or the abuse of other children;

- masquerading as a minor or assuming a false identity to deceive a child; and

- using school or hobby sites to gather information about a child's interests, likes and dislikes.

(UK Council for Child Internet Safety 2012, p.16)

Because of their lack of social skills, communication problems and unawareness of other people's intent or objectives, autistic children can be more vulnerable to online grooming. It is therefore extremely important that you teach your child how to spot the danger signs and what to watch out for.

> A US survey reported 42% of young people aged 10–17 being exposed to online pornography in a one-year period; 66% of this exposure was unwanted.
>
> (Department for Education 2011, p.4)

It is recommended that you research your own country's internet safety websites as these will often provide age-appropriate videos and presentations designed specifically for children to watch, which will (sometimes shockingly) show the dangers of the internet and Web.

Racism, hate, self-harm, suicide and gambling websites

> EU Kids Online (Livingstone *et al.* 2011) found that seeing violent or hateful content was the third most common risk to young people and had been experienced by approximately one third of teenagers.
>
> (Department for Education 2011, p.4)

Often children and teens can be inquisitive about websites or internet content that contain references to this type of subject matter, or they may be enticed by websites supporting harmful and/or precarious actions.

Autistic children and teens can be especially susceptible to misunderstanding these type of websites because they tend to take matters literally, so it is important that they are educated to distinguish 'facts' from 'opinions' – and ideally have your support for extra guidance on this matter if they continue to be unsure!

Does your autistic teen have access to a debit or credit card? Be very careful they do not venture into the world of online gambling websites, which will drain their bank account quickly and assume no responsibility. Remember, many autistic people have little awareness of money and are vulnerable to addiction. If you believe your child may be gambling you must act quickly. The recommendation would be only to allow your child to use their card online when you are present!

REAL-LIFE STORY – KIRSTY

Kirsty is a high-functioning autistic woman of 19 who is normally very mature and responsible in most areas of her life.

Last year, however, Kirsty began to show signs that she was struggling with her finances as she was often borrowing money from her mother, claiming that she had overspent on luxury items or had miscalculated her budget.

Kirsty's mother eventually became concerned enough to inspect bank statements, and found, much to her horror, that Kirsty had been spending all her money gambling in popular online bingo websites.

After much discussion, they decided on the following actions:

- to cut up and cancel all debit/credit cards and to go to the bank in the high street on a weekly basis and work with cash only

- to try to enlist the help of a local support group – or start one themselves!

- to install parental control software on the computer (which her mother set up and password protected).

Thankfully Kirsty has managed to stop gambling. Her mother and all those who support Kirsty understand that this is a problem that will need to be addressed regularly to prevent further addiction and should not be ignored.

If your child visits any of these types of websites it should motivate you to talk to your child immediately about the risks and dangers involved. Do not assume that the visit was just idle curiosity, made in error or a passing phase. Ask your child why they chose to visit these sites and find out the reason behind it.

Spam, email fraud and phishing

Spam is typically 'junk mail' sent by the use of electronic messaging systems and software programs indiscriminately, and to as many people as possible. The most commonly identified form of spam is email spam, but the term can also be applied to similar abuses in other media such as instant messaging. Spam can saturate your inbox with unsolicited messages and advertising, and your address and telephone numbers could be sold on, meaning you could be bombarded with annoying telemarketing calls and postal mail too.

Email fraud typically proposes get-rich-quick schemes or offers fictitious investment opportunities. An example of this is being contacted by a member of a wealthy family desperately trying to get a large amount of money out of a country such as Nigeria and seeking your help in return for a large share of the wealth. A common variation of this is a woman claiming to be newly widowed and that she wants to leave millions of dollars of her husband's estate to a charity or church. Victims are usually asked to cover small fees such as legal expenses in return for a large portion of this vast sum of money. However, they never see any of the promised money – because there isn't any! This scam is not even new; its variant dates back to the 1580s when it was known as 'The Spanish Prisoner' con. Such scams can often be recognised by their poor spelling and grammar, as in the following example. Here is a typical (and real) example of this type of scam.

EXAMPLE OF EMAIL FRAUD

Attention: Dear Fund Beneficiary;

This is to officially inform you that your fund of (USD $10.5M) is now ready to be delivered to you through an ATM Master Card We are so sorry for the delay for the past feel months, now we have been able to solve the problem that was holding your fund by the United Nation (UN), Please kindly reconfirm the information below for your payment and delivery.

Customer details:

1. Your full name:…

2. Your home address:…

3. Your cell phone number:…

4. Identity card or Passport:…

5. Occupation:…

Please note that you are going to pay for the Activation/ Insurance fee of your card which is $350 only. Your ATM Master card payment will be send to you through a Global Post Delivery service it takes 48hours to arrive.

A copy of your ATM card will be sent to you upon the receipt of your details and your payment slip of $350 for the ATM CARD activation and insurance, also note that your Pin code will be given to you through phone only.

So kindly get back to us with the above requirements to enable us proceed with your payment and delivery immediately

One again we sincerely apologies for the delay.

Phishing is the name given to online scams where criminals fraudulently acquire private information by masquerading as a recognised and trusted organisation, for example a bank, and by contacting victims directly via email or instant messaging, typically stating that there are security issues with an account and persuading the victim to respond with sensitive information. This private information can then be used for several illegal purposes, such as being sold to online advertisers.

Autistic children who receive spam or fraudulent emails may be less likely than others to detect that the message is not from who it claims to be and therefore are more likely to expose themselves to these types of threats.

Remember that your autistic child may not understand 'lies' the same way others do, so it is very important that you prevent your child from seeing these types of threats in the first place by installing a good firewall and both anti-virus and anti-spam software.

REAL-LIFE STORY – DANIEL

Daniel is 14 and likes to use the internet often. He was recently permitted by his parents to set up a new email address. After a few weeks he started to receive lots of unsolicited emails, which were very confusing to him.

One of these emails suggested that Daniel's bank account had security issues and that he should immediately visit (click through to) the relevant website and update his details.

Daniel's grandmother had set up a bank account for him when he was a small child and Daniel was aware of this fact, although he had no knowledge of how much money was in the account, or what it was for. All he understood from this email was that he had to contact the bank and update his details.

Because Daniel is autistic he has problems understanding lies and takes things literally, so he clicked the link in the email which directed him to the website of a bank. He then attempted to input his information but because he did not know the bank account number, Daniel could not complete the registration processes. It was only then, when he asked his parents to help him, that they discovered this was a phishing scam.

Although Daniel's parents deleted the unsolicited email, and explained to their son that this was in fact a scam called 'phishing', the damage had already been done and the computer had become infected with spyware which had to be removed by an anti-spyware software program with the aid of an expensive computer expert.

Daniel's parents now use anti-spam software, as well as anti-virus software, which removes the vast majority of junk mail before Daniel sees it, helping reduce frustration for their son. He also knows now not to click on *any* emails he receives which contain hyperlinks, unless his parents approve first.

Most internet browsers and email software packages these days also offer ways you can report spam, email fraud or phishing directly, so if your child's inbox is full of unwanted messages, take steps to prevent this occurring in the future and report anything you deem illegal.

Cyber-terrorism – threats to national and international security

Many websites these days, including government websites, contain or are networked to very important and highly sensitive data and information and even these, utilising the most sophisticated anti-virus and firewall technology available today, still have threats to their security. The reason for this is simply because some people are so inquisitive and/or want to empower themselves with the knowledge of undisclosed matters of national and international importance, that they continually try to find ways to access these websites.

Cyber-terrorism is the use of the internet to implement and execute deliberate large-scale disruption to computer networks using methods such as a computer virus to cause destruction and harm for personal objectives.

Today there is much concern about the potential damages that could be caused by acts of cyber-terrorism, and this has encouraged official responses from government agencies, authorities and media sources.

Online you can find unscrupulous hacker organisations and 'gangs' waiting to recruit your autistic child – especially those with good computer programming skills. These organisations claim only to be movements opposed to the computer security industry but some of the things they do are seen as illegal or indeed even acts of cyber-terrorism. You should be aware of these organisations so you can recognise any signs if your child should be contacted or become involved. For more on this subject see Chapter 8, Computer Hacking and Autism.

TWO SIMPLE STEPS TO ENSURE INTERNET SAFETY FOR YOUR FAMILY

1. Take the time and make the effort to *teach yourself* how to educate your child about the possible dangers of the internet and learn how to supervise their online activities. If you feel unsure about the technology, why not try a free IT or internet evening course somewhere or even ask a friend or family member to teach you? The more you know about computers and the internet, and the safety issues around them, the more you can safeguard your child.

2. Ensure you have a strong firewall and security protection for your network.

If you want to secure your home network effectively you will need:

- *A firewall* – this is a tool (can be hardware but more commonly these days it is in the form of software) that controls the flow of communication across networks of computers by examining the source, destination and type of communication and comparing these against prearranged databases of allowed or disallowed connections.

   You need a firewall because when you are online, your computer is continuously connected to the internet and identified by a unique number – the IP address – so it is potentially visible to anyone else on that network, and therefore malicious users may be able to gain access to it.

- *Anti-virus software* – this is a computer program that detects, prevents and takes action to deactivate or remove malicious software programs, such as viruses and worms. It is very important that your anti-virus software is kept up to date at all times because new threats are being created and executed precipitously and frequently.

- *Anti-spyware software* – this is a type of program designed to prevent and detect unwanted spyware program installations and to remove those programs if installed.

- *Anti-spam software* – this is the easiest way to check and manage your emails before you download them to your computer to ensure removal of spam and junk mail.

- *A robust password for wireless connections* – if your password is easy to remember or work out, change it to one that will be hard for others to detect – you do not want strangers logged into your home network!

Making the internet child-safe is also possible with the help of certain additional security software and/or hardware, which is discussed in Chapter 3.

A note to parents/carers: The internet can be an extremely valuable and helpful educational tool as well as an engaging and interactive form of communication and entertainment for your autistic child. Given the right circumstances, and with strong guidance, teaching and support, your child can benefit greatly by making use of this amazing modern technology. The positive aspects *do* far outweigh the negative, but only if parents and carers take internet safety issues seriously and take regular interest/action.

CHAPTER 3

Strategies for the Parent/Carer and Solutions to Problems

INTRODUCTION

Unfortunately, as discussed earlier in this book, there are numerous potential risks and dangers to your child while they are online – either on the internet or the Web. Please be assured, however, that these threats can be reduced with a combination of modern technology and good parenting.

In this chapter the aim is to provide you with information, strategies and options to help you help your autistic child.

Please remember that you should never rely on a single solution or approach. Your autistic child is an individual and therefore some of this chapter content will be irrelevant or not suitable for your child. The boundaries you decide to set and the kind of conversations you have with your child will depend on their age and technical ability. Also remember that circumstances will change as your child grows up and this should be reconsidered regularly and accordingly.

Figure 3.1 Strategies for parents/carers

Be confident

Your child's computer, no matter who purchased it, is *your* property until they turn 18.

Do not be fooled or bullied/intimidated into believing you are breaking a law or doing anything wrong by asking to view your child's computer, laptop or mobile phone when it suits you. This also applies if you decide to take the equipment away, whether to protect your child if you are suspicious of misuse, or for punishment purposes. You should feel confident in the knowledge that the computer or device is *your* property.

Be curious

The next step is to *communicate* with your autistic child and to learn as much as you can about their computer use to help keep them safe online.

Communicating with your child and setting boundaries are part of keeping them safe online. Become a detective, question your child in a calm discussion about their computer use, and take notes for future reference.

Example questions:

- What do they use the computer for?
- What are their favourite software packages?
- What is their email address and password?
- What websites do they visit and prefer?
- Whom (if anyone) do they talk to online?
- What are their user name(s) and password(s) for the websites they use?
- What is the method they use to communicate with others online (e.g. chat room)?

You may not get all the answers to your questions immediately, but if you repeat the questions over a period of time and take notes you will eventually build up a portfolio of your child's computer use.

It is advisable to re-ask your child these questions on a regular basis (every three months, for example), as these will change frequently. If you keep a note of the answers as suggested you have the knowledge you need to view and research the various websites at your convenience, thus ensuring that your child's computer use is acceptable and they are free from harm.

You can get an immediate idea of the websites your child is visiting by checking the 'browser history' in the browser software they use. When your child visits a website it is saved in the browser history and is available to view (unless your child has deleted or removed the list).

Be cautious

The only real way a parent/carer can help their autistic child to use a computer safely is by understanding the potential risks involved themselves and by being knowledgeable about what their child is doing online.

The threats to your child online are very real – so please be extremely cautious before allowing your child to use a computer.

The more you understand your child's computer use the easier it will be for you to monitor this and safeguard your child. If you are unaware of the potential risks or do not have the know-how to supervise and monitor your child's computer use, you will unfortunately be unable to support and encourage this important medium for your child.

Be prepared

The first thing to do is to decide, communicate and agree what your child *can* and *cannot* do online. The key to your child having a good online experience is for you to set rules, boundaries and limits, and for you to set these down in writing, or pictures if necessary. Remember, the clearer your rules are, the easier it will be for your autistic child to understand and follow them.

WHAT YOU CAN DO TO KEEP YOUR CHILD SAFE ONLINE
Warn them about strangers

As difficult as it may seem at times, your job as a parent/carer is to protect your child, and this sometimes means discussing difficult terms, topics or situations, such as strangers. In a calm and clear way, explain to your autistic child that people they do not already know are 'strangers' and this can be offline or online. Also teach them that strangers are sometimes not necessarily who they say they are, and 'bad' people can and do appear to be friendly and 'good'. Explain that these 'bad' people use online areas such as social networking websites to try to talk to vulnerable people in order to exploit them in some manner. Understanding this will be extremely challenging for the autistic child but you must persevere.

The key rule to teach your child is simple: 'Only have friends that you know and trust in the real world.'

An easier way may be to try explaining the threats around your child's favourite toy, hobby or story, or use fairy tales such as *Snow White and the Seven Dwarfs* (where the wicked stepmother is a bad person online who tries to get Snow White through the internet rather than directly with the poisonous apple). The more personal you make it, the easier it will be for your autistic child to understand and acknowledge the potential threats.

Please remember that although this can be frightening for your child, the benefits of computers and the scope of possibilities that this medium offers are so high that it is important they are taught certain rules. Focus on this positive aspect, when in doubt about allowing your child to use a computer and worrying about their safety.

Set a password on your child's computer so that only you can log onto it, or password protect your 'router'

If you set up your computer-operating software so that only your password is effective to start up the system, your child will have to ask you to log on in order to use it. This can be very effective for times when you are out of the house, for example.

However, this may not be practical for older children, who may want to use the computer for homework, or for the more computer literate child, who may find ways around the security of the password.

You can also change the password on your router. Your 'router' is the piece of hardware supplied to you normally by your ISP (internet service provider) when you sign up with them. This is the hardware that connects your phone line or cable to your computer, allowing internet access.

Routers are typically wireless these days, meaning that there is no need for any devices to be cabled to the router.

When you set up your router you are normally supplied with a password for your network and this is often written on a card or on a sticker on the underside of the device. This is the password needed to connect, for example, a laptop.

It is recommended that you change this password. If your child's laptop cannot connect to the home network because they do not know the password, they can still utilise and benefit from their laptop by doing other things with it, such as keeping a diary.

You can find out more information on changing the password of your router from your ISP.

Make sure you and your child know how to block messages and/or users

Also remember that you will have to teach yourself and your child how to block messages and/or other website users and it is important that you know the actions you need to take should someone approach/try to 'friend' your child. (More information can be found on this in Chapter 6, Social Media.)

> Compared to 2012, children are less likely to know how to block messages from someone they don't want to hear from (53% vs. 68%) and to have done this in the past year (32% vs. 42%).
>
> (Ofcom 2013b, p.8)

Make it explicitly clear that your child must never disclose personal information

You must educate your child to know *never* to give out addresses, phone numbers, school details, passwords or photographs/videos to any strangers or upload to websites they do not recognise or have never heard of.

If your child is filling out biographies or profiles, for example, ensure that they leave fields blank and explain that there is no need for them to post personal information in this way.

If you ask your child if they would give their telephone number or a photograph of themselves to a man on the street, the answer will usually be 'no'. Explain to your autistic child that this rule should also apply to everyone they meet online.

And remember, even if your child does not disclose personal information on, for example, social networking websites, if they were to upload an innocent photograph of themselves dressed in their school uniform, a paedophile may be able to identify the school and find your child.

Explain the differences between 'fact' and 'opinion'

Many autistic people take things literally, whether said verbally or in written form, and learning to understand the differences is a valuable skill.

There are so many websites available and easily accessible which allow people to view and share their opinions these days. This is challenging for the autistic child and must be addressed.

Explain to your child the differences and understand how challenging this is for your child. Encourage your child to ask you for confirmation if in doubt whether something might be fact or simply someone else's opinion on a subject.

REAL-LIFE STORY – STACY

Stacy is a 15-year-old autistic girl who always takes things literally. She has high-functioning autism and was lucky enough to get a laptop at Christmas as she is very good with computers. After a short period of time, Stacy's parents noticed that she had become agitated with her laptop and was in a general bad mood. Her parents inspected her laptop and discovered that Stacy had been visiting web forums and posting 'rude' comments in response to someone's opinion on a specific subject. The original commentator had quickly responded with a rude reply and the backlash was difficult for Stacy to understand.

After her parents had discussed their find with Stacy, it became apparent that she did not understand the difference between someone's opinions on a subject and the actual facts relevant to that subject. This left her feeling extremely confused and angry – hence her rude comments.

Her parents discussed with Stacy exactly what opinions were and why they differed from fact and are working with Stacy to continue to teach her the difference. Before posting comments on any forum, Stacy will now ask her parents to proofread her messages and they all share their 'opinions' on the subject at hand before she hits 'submit'.

Stacy is no longer angry with online strangers and enjoys sharing her own views on the Web.

Plan ahead before allowing your child to use the computer.

Set tasks for your child to do to encourage safe use such as playing games. If you sit your child in front of the computer and leave them to it you can expect problems. There are so many 'bad' things for them to see and do and if left unattended, and even without directly searching, they are bound to stumble across some illegal content. Take matters into your own hands by setting tasks for them to do.

Take the time to plan your child's computer use. If you allow your child to use the computer for two hours at a time, for example, then set tasks you know will fill this time. Tasks such as games, diary keeping, word processing and using creative artistic software are all helpful suggestions.

REAL-LIFE STORY – JESSICA

Jessica is a 14-year-old girl with low-functioning autism. Her family live on a tight budget and have not afforded a home computer until recently. She has been unsure and a bit scared of computers and technology from a young age when using them in school and, unlike most children, did not want to use the computer when the family installed one at home. Her parents tried to show her how to use the computer but Jessica became upset and frequently broke the mouse out of frustration. Her parents were concerned that she would not benefit from the help of computers in her life.

Since she was a young child, however, Jessica has had a fascination with dressing up dolls. This hobby, unfortunately for the family, was becoming a very expensive one and putting a strain on family finances, as Jessica would be violent and abusive if she did not frequently get a new doll and accessories.

With her parents' advanced planning, help and support, Jessica registered with a free children's games website which hosts various simple-to-use and colourful games where the player can 'cyberly' dress a wide variety of dolls in a choice of hundreds of different costumes.

Jessica became quickly skilled at using the game software and her mouse skills dramatically improved.

Jessica's parents now plan their daughter's computer activities and use this medium to encourage and motivate her with her homework and develop other skills such as hand–eye co-ordination. If Jessica carries out her set tasks in a timely way she is allowed to spend one hour a day on the doll website. Not only did this family save money on the cost of doll's clothes and accessories, Jessica now understands that she can only get dolls for special occasions such as birthdays and Christmas. She is more than happy with her 'cyber-dollies'.

Research age-appropriate websites that you can recommend to your child

Age-appropriate websites contain far more security than normal websites and usually have limited functionality suitable for children. Normally the content on these websites has been designed and aimed specifically for children under certain ages. There are many excellent websites your child can take advantage of. Search for these websites in your browser and bookmark the age-relevant ones for future use. Remember to explore and check the options and security features of the websites before you introduce them to your child.

Set time limits

Time limits, especially for autistic children, are essential. Think back to when you were a child – if permitted to sit all day in front of a computer with all its functions and colours and sounds and abilities, would you get 'lost' in time? Most children, if left to their own devices, will sit in front of a computer all day long. It is your job as a good parent to ensure this does not happen.

The most common dangers of prolonged or addictive computer use are described in more detail in Chapter 4, Computer/Gaming Addiction and the Autistic Child, with health issues, such as joint and muscle problems, Carpal Tunnel Syndrome and vision problems being some of the main dangers.

There are many software programs (usually now included within operating systems) that will allow parents to set time limits on their child's computer use. The computer will simply shut down after a set duration or can be set on timer mode to come on at a certain time and go off again at a certain time throughout the day.

Think about where the computer is located

It is best not to allow your child to have a computer in their own bedroom as this makes it more difficult to monitor and therefore safeguard your child. Insist that the computer is in a shared room in the house, with the screen visible at all times.

Install parental control software

Most computers these days come with operating systems, such as Windows, which include basic firewalls and parental control software. This may be enough for the majority of parents and carers, but if you want extra protection you should also consider installing additional parent control software.

Inexpensive commercial parental control software available today will normally record:

- all keystrokes and capture every single word your child types
- all chats and messages – both sides of the conversation
- emails sent and received
- every website your child visits and what they do while on them
- everything your child does and sees on social networking websites (including all the profiles they visit and pictures they post)
- online searches.

Parental control software will sometimes also allow you to:

- remotely review the recordings from another PC or Mac
- see every program your child runs on the computer, including games and software
- be notified when your child uses inappropriate language or visits inappropriate websites
- block your child from visiting websites you deem inappropriate
- block your child from chatting with anyone.

It is therefore very important that you consider purchasing and installing this type of software. It is not spying on your child, nor is it illegal – remember, the computer they use legally belongs to you until they reach the age of 18, so be confident and decisive in your choice!

REAL-LIFE STORY – SCOTT

Scott is a high-functioning autistic boy who has a superb aptitude for computing. His parents became concerned when Scott started showing signs of addiction, spending hours in his room, hiding his monitor screen when his parents tried to look at what he was doing and becoming very agitated.

His parents purchased and installed additional parental control software and using this found that their son had been penning racist remarks and being abusive towards individuals on a social networking site. Much to their horror, this had gone on to the extent that he had been banned from one particular website.

When confronted he became extremely upset and did not understand the consequences of his actions.

Eventually his parents discovered that Scott's action had been the result of overhearing his peers at school and literally believing the racist comments made against an Asian student.

Without this parental control software his parents would have been unlikely to find the cause of Scott's change in personality and to address this issue quickly.

With the help of a 'Social Stories' lesson, and his school, Scott learned why racism is not acceptable. Scott's parents then decided to move his computer into the lounge, only enabling Scott to use it when they were in the room.

Make sure your child understands that you are there to support them

Many autistic children find it extremely difficult to ask for help so you should take the time to make it clear to your child that they must come to you if they see anything online that makes them feel uneasy, uncomfortable, threatened or something they simply don't understand.

Your child needs to be confident that they won't be in trouble and that sharing their online worries or experiences is a good thing. Remember that online 'predators' are sometimes very skilful at making those they try to build a relationship with, groom or abuse, feel guilty and responsible. They also have ways to manipulate the child into doing things they normally would not do and to keep quiet, such as saying they know where the child lives and they will hurt parents or siblings. The child can be made to feel unsafe and dirty, so they need to know that you are there for them for support and guidance and not to judge harshly their actions.

Explain to your child: 'The person who did/said this to you is responsible – not you.'

Absolutely forbid your child to meet online contacts in person
It is understandable that your child may want to meet their new 'friend' face to face, but to keep your child safe you must insist that they never meet someone in person whom they have encountered online without your consent and a responsible adult present.

REAL-LIFE STORY – BRUCE

Bruce is a high-functioning autistic boy of 12. He loves football. On a football fan website he was approached by a boy called Simon who was of a similar age. The two boys chatted online regularly, eventually exchanging personal information such as phone numbers.

When Simon asked to meet him face to face to play a game of football, Bruce was very excited. Bruce was convinced Simon was who he claimed to be – after all, Simon had shared photographs over the internet of himself playing football and in his school uniform and with other friends. Bruce had never discussed this issue with his parents before so he did not think to tell them about the meeting.

On the day of the meeting Bruce was very excited and made his way to the address Simon had given him. He knocked on the door and it was answered by a man in his late twenties claiming to be Simon's older brother. He indicated that Simon had 'popped out' to the shops and that Bruce should come in and wait. He seemed friendly and unthreatening.

Unfortunately, in this instance, Bruce went into the house to wait for his new friend where it quickly became clear that 'Simon' was fictitious – a character made up by a desperate paedophile enticing young boys into his home via the internet.

If your child continues to insist on meeting someone whom they have encountered online:

- ask to talk to the child/person concerned directly
- ask to talk to the parents of that child/person directly
- if all seems safe, arrange to take your child to a large public place, such as a busy park, for the meeting
- do not leave the two children together alone – always keep an eye on them!
- set a time limit for the initial meeting.

Explain what computer viruses and spyware are

A computer virus is typically a small computer program created specifically to cause harm to your computer or to gather valuable personal information such as user names and passwords, and has the ability to replicate itself and spread to other computers.

Malware and spyware programs such as worms and Trojan horses act like viruses and can also harm your computer system, but most do not have the ability to reproduce themselves like viruses.

A virus or malware/spyware can be very costly and inconvenient because, if infected, your computer may become extremely slow in performance, or even disrupted to such an extent that the hard drive may have to be reformatted or even replaced – as well as the computer being exposed to other potential threats.

You should teach your child about the different types of computer viruses, the damage they can potentially do to the computer they use and why it is important never to click a link in an email or instant message as this is the most common way people get viruses.

If you do not have anti-virus software installed on the computer your child uses they will be vulnerable to all sorts of threats, so please download and install either a free basic anti-virus software package or consider buying one and/or upgrading your existing software.

Agree with your child whether or not they are allowed to spend money online

If your child is over a certain age they may have access to a debit or credit card. It is certainly not recommended to allow your child to use their debit or credit card online. Not only does this open up security issues, such as fraud, but your autistic child may find it impossible *not* to buy certain items they like or be lured into buying things they really don't need or want.

However, if you do decide to allow your child to spend money online, make sure that they know to shop only at well-known reputable websites and that they know what to look out for to prevent their card details falling into the wrong hands. Set a monetary limit and agree that they must never go over this without your permission.

Remember to tell them *never* to give out their card details to anyone online who asks for them and, if they are in doubt about any transaction, to come to you immediately.

It is wise at this point to remember that you will have to amend your rules, boundaries and limits as your child gets older as factors will change over time.

TASKS

1. Ask your child to write down or record the answers to these questions:
   - What do they use the computer for?
   - Which websites do they visit and prefer?
   - Whom (if anyone) do they talk to online?
   - Have they ever been contacted by a stranger online?
   - What are their user name(s) and password(s) for the websites they use?
   - What is the method they use to communicate with others online (e.g. chat room)?
   - Do they know what viruses and spyware are?
   - What else would they like to be able to do on the computer?
   - Any other questions you feel are relevant.

2. Ask your child to join a children's website and watch what information they feel they need to give out and then discuss what, if in the wrong hands, could be done with this information.

3. Dedicate at least an hour of your time, whether this is in your lunch hour or in an evening, to research age-appropriate websites that you can suggest to your child. There are great free websites out there that will help your child develop a wide range of skills, so why not make the most of them?

4. Spend some time getting to know what firewall and anti-virus software you have currently installed on your child's computer. If it is inadequate, research and purchase accordingly and also consider purchasing one of the various commercial parental control software packages available online at the same time.

5. Consider a structure where your child earns their computer time. For example, for each homework assignment completed correctly they would receive a 15-minute computer time slot. Create this timetable using your computer or use the sample in Appendix 2 of this book.

6. Complete the Computer Information Form in Appendix 2 of this book alongside your child to get a better understanding of their knowledge of computers.

CHAPTER 4

Computer/Gaming Addiction and the Autistic Child

INTRODUCTION

It is only recently that the term 'computer/internet addiction' has come into use. Computer addicts often show negative behaviours similar to those of other known addictive disorder sufferers and it, too, can unfortunately control and wreck lives.

Parents and carers of autistic children need to be very careful – if left unsupervised, some children can develop bad habits in computer use that can cause significant problems in other areas of their lives.

Debates are currently ongoing about whether or not excessive use of the computer and/or the internet is an actual addiction, but it seems very clear that the potential risks and dangers for children are there and should be addressed.

There are various types of computer or internet addicts. Texas State University's Counseling Center outlines the following five types:

1. *Computer addict* – someone who is obsessed with playing computer games and/or with computer programming.

2. *Cybersex addict* – someone who obsessively uses internet pornography, adult chat rooms and/or adult websites for sexual satisfaction.

3. *Cyber-relationship addict* – someone with an addiction to social networking websites, chat rooms and messaging to such an extent that online 'friends' become more important than real-life relationships.

4. *Net compulsion addict* – someone with an addiction to online shopping, gambling or auction sites, such as bingo or QVC online shopping.

5. *Information overload addict* – someone who compulsively surfs the Web or searches databases.

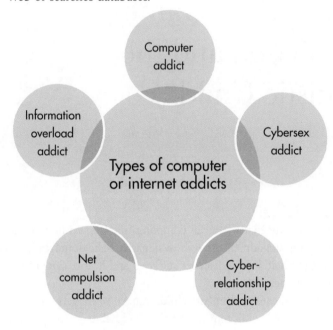

Figure 4.1 Types of computer or internet addicts

WHY ARE AUTISTIC CHILDREN MORE AT RISK OF DEVELOPING AN ADDICTION?

> Boys with ASD spend much more time playing video games than do boys with TD,[1] and boys with ASD and ADHD are at greater risk for problematic video game use than are boys with TD.
> (Mazurek and Engelhardt 2013, p.260)

Most autistic children enjoy simple, repetitive tasks and this can be achieved by the use of a computer – whether it be gaming or using other software – where rewards/targets are often easily achieved. Because many autistic children also feel reprieved from stress when using a computer,

---

1   TD: typical development.

it could become so enjoyable that it could increase the risk of your child becoming addicted.

Because autistic children may be withdrawn, solitary, easily bored, or even suffer from an additional addiction or impulse control disorder, they can be especially vulnerable to computer addiction or overuse.

DETERMINE IF YOUR CHILD HAS AN ADDICTION

Do you think your autistic child may have a computer addiction? If so, take steps now.

Have a discussion with your child immediately and ask them the following questions (as you deem appropriate):

- When you are not on your computer, how often do you think about it?
- Do you lose track of time while on the computer?
- How do you feel if your computer time is limited?
- Have you ever hurried a task so you can get back to your computer?
- Do you have any problems in school because you spend too much time using your computer and not enough time on school work?
- Do your feelings ever transfer between happiness and guilt while using your computer?
- Have you ever lied to your family or friends about the amount of time you spend on the computer and what you do while on it?
- Do you spend more of your time talking to online friends, instead of friends at school or college?
- Do you think you spend too much time on the computer?
- Have you ever tried to limit your computer use in the past?

The answers to these questions will give you a very good indication if your child has a problem, and if you think they do, then please act immediately. As a parent, it is your role to ensure that you help to break your child's computer addiction before it causes physical, emotional and intellectual damage.

WHAT TO DO IF YOU FEEL YOUR CHILD MAY HAVE AN ADDICTION

Start off by making a note of the hours and minutes your child spends using a computer over a period of one week. (See Appendix 2 of this book for a Child's Computer Log – Hours Per Week Form.) Many parents will be surprised and shocked by the results. Anything over 12 hours per week (the current average) should give you cause for concern.

If your autistic child is under stress they may only be using the computer excessively to help relieve this. Other disorders, such as depression or anxiety, may be the actual cause of the overuse of computers. If you think or suspect this may be the case with your child, contact your GP for more advice.

Support groups specifically designed for addiction can be very helpful but are hard to find, especially for children. If you cannot find a suitable support group, consider setting one up with your child who could invite other school students or friends who are trying to regain control over their computer use. You do get online support counsellors but getting your child out of the house and away from the computer and in a relaxed setting is paramount.

Try to get your child to admit that they have a computer obsession/ addiction or overuse problem. If your child understands that they have a problem it is the first step to them overcoming that problem. Explain to your autistic child that there is no use in avoiding the truth, it is a common problem and you are there to help them. Your autistic child should not be made to feel ashamed or embarrassed in any way about their addiction as this can have very negative consequences.

Keeping a Child's Computer Activity Log (see sample available in Appendix 2) can help you and your autistic child understand their feelings when using their computer and/or the internet.

These simple plans can help to assess how the computer affects your autistic child's mood and track if and when your child's moods change to help you identify potential problems.

HOW TO HELP YOUR ADDICTED CHILD

- Be a good role model. Make sure you (and other family members) manage your own computer use well. You cannot expect your child not to learn addiction directly from you if they see you constantly using a computer.

- Limit your child's time on the computer and consider moving the system to a shared room if possible.

- Turn off mobile phones – especially those with an internet connection – at a certain time each evening, for example 8pm, so your child cannot text or surf the Web.

- Physically collect all laptops, phones and technology gadgets at a certain time each evening and keep them stored safely in a family room overnight, such as your bedroom.

- Get your autistic child out of the house and involved in non-computer-related fun and activities. Addictions are extremely hard to break and it will be even harder for your autistic child if they have nothing else to occupy their spare time.

- If you know any other children who use computers sensibly consider introducing your child to them as sharing and exchanging experiences with other children will help make your autistic child think about their own computer use.

- Assign your child extra chores or take away other privileges if they continue to overuse the computer.

WHAT OTHER HARM CAN COMPUTER ADDICTION DO?

As well as the emotional problems associated with computer addiction, your autistic child is also at risk of the following physical problems:

- back and neck ache
- Carpal Tunnel Syndrome (pain, numbness and burning in the hands that can crawl up to the wrists, elbows and shoulders)
- strained vision or dry eyes
- severe headaches or migraines
- disturbances in sleep pattern.

For more information read Chapter 10 where we discuss how to adapt your child's workstation area and other health and safety issues.

REAL-LIFE STORY – MARTIN

Martin is a 17-year-old boy who has autism. He started using computers in school when he was 12 and very much enjoyed surfing the Web and searching for general information.

When he was 15 he was given a laptop but within six months his parents started noticing changes in their son:

- He began to sleep all day, missing school, and staying up all night.

- He would suffer from migraine headaches regularly and complained of general aches and pains.

- His behaviour deteriorated and he started having tantrums/moods which were difficult for his parents to control.

Martin's parents noticed that their son was using his laptop a bit too much and they decided to find out what he was doing on the device. Using the internet to help, they downloaded and installed parental control software onto Martin's laptop and found that he was spending literally hours and hours daily searching nothing but news websites. They agreed that their son was probably suffering from information overload addiction and they needed to take action.

First they decided that set time limits were required for Martin's laptop. Initially, it was extremely difficult as Martin was determined to use the laptop all the time, but gradually he began to appreciate the time he did get to go online.

Martin's health and behaviour improved quickly and he was back to his old self within a few weeks.

CHAPTER 5

Cyberbullying

INTRODUCTION

> Bullying is a relational problem involving repetitive, negative actions directed toward a student, and characterized by a power imbalance — physical, social, cognitive, between the victim and perpetrator.
>
> (Olweus 1993)

A cyberbully is the term given to someone (a child or an adult) who employs modern-day technology to bully — that is, hurt, humiliate, discredit or embarrass another person.

Cyberbullying is a relatively new safety concern but unfortunately has already been the cause of teen suicides and is becoming an ever-increasing problem for the younger child and for adults too.

Some facts about cyberbullying

> Between 8% and 34% of children and young people in the UK have been cyberbullied, and girls are twice as likely to experience persistent cyberbullying than boys.
>
> (Department for Education 2011, p.3)

Most children these days see computers and mobile phones as positive tools that help them develop their individual identities and that encourage social networking, allowing them to feel connected to their peers.

Unfortunately, there is a flip-side to this as modern technology can also be used negatively and inappropriately. As technology such as computers and mobile phones becomes increasingly popular, the misuse of this technology will also rise.

CYBERBULLYING AND AUTISM

> Over 90 per cent of parents of children with Asperger Syndrome reported that their child had been bullied in the previous 12 months.
>
> (Little 2002)

The majority of bullies pick on people they see as different or less advantaged than themselves. Children with learning disabilities and at mainstream school are victimised more than neurotypical children because they often show signs of being out of the ordinary, especially when it comes to social cues and communication.

Most autistic children will simply not recognise cyberbullying as a form of bullying, even if they have been taught and understand the concept of the schoolyard bully.

The autistic child may feel very alone and misunderstood and may not believe that the adults who support them will understand or identify it as a problem either.

Be alert! If your child seems overly upset or agitated after using the internet or their mobile phone, it might be an indication of cyberbullying.

HOW CYBERBULLYING STARTS

Cyberbullying usually starts when a child (or a group of children) sends a callous message to another child using modern technology. If and/or when that child gets caught, instead of stopping the bullying immediately, they learn how to disguise their online identities by using fake email addresses or instant messaging accounts and the cyberbullying can escalate – often with the attacks becoming more sophisticated and intimidating.

The cyberbully may even begin to pose as the victim on forums or social media sites and reveal highly embarrassing or private information. They may even make up and post false information online to discredit and hurt their victim. These cyberbullies have also been known to use image- or video-editing software to create reputation-ruining, indecent and fake pictures or videos of their victim and then post them online. What is even more worrying is that the attacker may post online personal information about your child, such as their home address, enabling paedophiles and other dangerous criminals to easily find your child.

Unfortunately, cyberbullying is something even the best computer security cannot protect against. Until someone comes up with a practical solution, the only protection your autistic child has against potential attackers is for you to understand what cyberbullying is, how to identify if your child is under threat, and what to do if it happens to them.

THE EFFECTS OF BULLYING

The effects of bullying can and have been extremely serious and even fatal. Victims can suffer from long-term emotional and behavioural problems. Bullying and cyberbullying can cause depression, anxiety, an increased susceptibility to illness, and can lead to low self-esteem.

REAL-LIFE STORY – RACHEL

At 15, Rachel believed she was well aware of the internet and any risks involved. Her parents had sat down with her often to go over the dangers of the internet and she knew what websites not to visit, and what links in emails not to click on.

Rachel has Asperger syndrome but is high functioning enough to go to mainstream school. One day a boy she vaguely knew stopped and started to chat to her and asked her out on a date. She was very happy – her first date!

Unfortunately, the boy was nothing but a bully surrounded by friends who had 'dared' him to ask Rachel out on a date. The boy in question obviously did not turn up for their date, and Rachel found on a social network website that the whole school was aware of the 'dare' and was laughing at her.

Rachel was so upset, hurt and confused that she felt she wanted to die and cut her wrists that night.

However, to make matters worse, Rachel took photographs of her cut and bloody wrists and posted them on the social media website in question. Needless to say, instead of sympathy coming her way and an explanation to the lies she had been told, Rachel received further bullying solely because of the pictures she had posted.

Even more people cruelly laughed at her, and her photographs were circulated to an even wider audience.

Fortunately, after much involvement from her parents, professionals and her school, Rachel has almost overcome this experience, but refuses to log onto any social media websites now or to chat to boys she does not know and trust.

WHAT IS THE DIFFERENCE BETWEEN BULLYING AND CYBERBULLYING?

Cyberbullying can be even worse than typical bullying because:

- Places that were previously regarded as secure or personal, such as the home, are now not safe havens.

- Cyberbullying can occur 24 hours a day/seven days a week.

- Most children who cyberbully do so anonymously and/or use fake identities so the victim does not even know who the bully actually is.

- Cyberbullying can occur across generations, with adults/teachers known to have been victims. Age and status is not always taken into account.

- Naïve or innocent children can become an accessory to the cyberbullying. They could, for example, innocently forward a message and therefore become involved in the situation.

- A wide audience to read offensive messages or fake posts can be reached quickly and easily, motivating and/or encouraging the cyberbully to continue with their actions.

STRATEGIES TO HELP YOUR CHILD COPE WITH CYBERBULLYING

There are various strategies you can use to help your child cope and deal with cyberbullying:

- Make sure your child is fully aware that they need to be very careful who they give email addresses, phone numbers and other such personal information to.

- Ensure your child understands that if the cyberbullying is taking place on a school or community website, they should do as they would do if the bullying was face to face – tell someone like you or a teacher.

- Explain to your child that it is best if they tell you immediately of any messages that are abusive or obscene and make sure they understand not to reply to them. If your child does not take time off to calm down they may end up writing something they will regret later and which may make the situation even worse.

- If the cyberbullying continues then you or a supporting adult need to find out where the messages are coming from.

- Collect evidence. Deleting messages may seem the easiest and quickest way to deal with the situation, but if the bullying escalates and becomes serious you should save or print the messages so that if you do need to take action in the future you have the appropriate evidence at hand.

- If your child is experiencing cyberbullying via a website, contact that website or source of attack and request they look into the situation. If necessary, lodge a formal complaint and attach a copy of any evidence with your letter.

WHAT ELSE CAN YOU DO?

- Contact your ISP (internet service provider) and request they help you with your complaint.

- The Internet Watch Foundation[1] will accept reports of abusive websites, particularly child pornography.

- The Child Exploitation and Online Protection Centre (CEOP) has advice and tips to help you, as well as letting you report online abuse.[2]

WHAT ELSE IS BEING DONE?

At the moment, most governments are researching solutions to this epidemic. New laws and regulations are coming into force annually, and new resources and information are being made available to parents and teachers.

Until something can be done to stop completely your child being at risk of cyberbullying while using the internet, you should not only educate your child about exactly what it is and what to look out for, but always ensure that they have a good firewall and anti-virus software as well as parental controls installed on the computer they use.

---

1   www.iwf.org.uk
2   http://ceop.police.uk

CHAPTER 6

Social Media, Including Blogging, Chat Rooms, Instant Messaging and Webcams

WHAT IS 'SOCIAL MEDIA'?

This term 'social media' is used to describe websites and online/mobile software/tools which enable people to interact with each other – by sharing information, opinions, knowledge and interests.

Social media makes it easy for people to listen, network, engage and collaborate with each other online.

Over the last four to five years, social networking has become a major part of young people's lives.

62% of all 5–16 year olds visited a social networking site in the last week. The figure for 2012–13 was 65%, and 74% the year before that, so the proportion using has fallen (mainly due to decline in Facebook use).

Amongst 9–16 year olds who go online (most of them), 73% have a profile on a social network, and 79% visited a social networking site in the last week.

(Childwise 2013–2014)

And parents beware – it is not only computers and laptops where a child can access social media platforms.

> Four in ten (41%) 12–15s with an active profile say they mostly use a mobile phone to visit their main social networking site profile – which makes this the most popular device for accessing their profiles.
>
> (Ofcom 2013b, p.6)

HISTORY OF SOCIAL MEDIA

By the 1970s, networking technology had advanced rapidly and in 1979 a company called UseNet gave its subscribers the tools needed to communicate to each other via an electronic newsletter.

In the 1980s, home computers were becoming more common and sophisticated and this applied to social media too. In the late 1980s, Internet Relay Chats (typically a service that allows participants to 'chat' in a live forum online) were first used and continued to be popular well into the 1990s.

In 1997, a website named Six Degrees was launched and this is usually acknowledged as the first social media website. This innovative website allowed users to upload a biography/profile and make friends with other users.

The first blogging websites became available in the late 1990s and still remain popular today.

By 2006, popular social media websites such as Facebook and Twitter had become available and these websites still remain some of the most popular social networking tools today.

Because of the faster broadband connections now available, social networking sites are easier and more interesting to use, as a faster connection allows more inventive use of the site, such as streaming videos and music, as well as performing basic tasks quickly and easily, such as uploading photos.

There is a huge variety of social networking websites available nowadays. Many of them can even be linked or connected to other social media websites to allow multiple or cross-posting. This enables users to reach more contacts/people easily, without sacrificing the personal touch.

WHY DO CHILDREN ENJOY USING SOCIAL MEDIA WEBSITES?

Children enjoy social media websites for many reasons, for example:

- They are more easily able to self-express and explore their identity.
- They can socialise with their friends.

- They enjoy being informed and being kept up to date on the latest news about their friends, relatives and peer groups.
- They can collaborate easily with their peers on school work.
- They can give or receive emotional support.
- It helps them with learning in an informal setting.
- It helps them discover and explore alternative interests.

WHY DO AUTISTIC CHILDREN ENJOY USING SOCIAL MEDIA WEBSITES?

As well as the above reasons, because computers and social networking mean it's easy to make friends or communicate with others without face-to-face contact, they prove to be a valuable resource for children on the autism spectrum because they allow these children to have conversations without the typical stresses/challenges normally faced when attempting to communicate.

WHAT ARE THE RISKS INVOLVED WITH SOCIAL MEDIA?

Children with a social networking site profile that may be visible to people not known to them are more likely to have undertaken some kind of potentially risky online behaviour, such as adding people to their contacts they don't know in person, or sending photos or personal details to people only known online.

(Ofcom 2013b, p.8)

You need also to teach/remind your child to be aware that social media websites frequently change their default privacy settings unsystematically and without giving their members prior notice. When this happens, private information and details are publicly available to find via search engines such as Google, enabling people to easily find your child!

Cyberbullying is the most common risk for children when using social media (for more information on cyberbullying see Chapter 5). It is important, therefore, for you to teach your child not to post any messages or chat to someone online in anger or on impulse and always to think before they post anything as these messages are extremely difficult to take back. It is also very important that your child knows to come to you if they feel bullied or harassed in any way.

Money transfer scams on social media websites are increasing. In some cases people have been tricked into transferring money to a friend or relative who has asked for help via a social media website, only to discover later that the friend's social media account had been hacked and they did not send any such request for help. If your child has a credit/debit card make sure they know never to give the card details out to anyone and also make sure they know never to transfer money to anyone without your permission – even if it is a very close friend or relative.

Other risks include 'clickjacking'. This is the term given when a seemingly harmless post with a link to enticing content redirects the user to a site that installs malware or spyware on their device.

'Likejacking' is the term given when a hacker controls your account and makes it look like you 'like' a website or someone else's post.

Fake applications can also put the child at risk, so you should also be vigilant against these. These are typically small programs not supported by the social media website, such as, 'see who viewed your timeline'. You should make sure your child is aware of these and avoids using them!

> When looking at the responses for children aged 8–12 with an active profile on Facebook/Bebo/MySpace, more than one in four of these children talk to people who are potentially not directly known to them (22%).
>
> (Ofcom 2013a, p.95)

REAL-LIFE STORY – MICHAEL

Michael is a 12-year-old high-functioning autistic boy who has recently been very depressed after the divorce of his parents. He has above average skills with computers and has a laptop in his bedroom.

One night he mentioned on a social networking website that he was feeling suicidal, and instead of support being offered from friends and peers, he was actually encouraged to commit suicide in front of the camera and before a potentially wide audience. Thankfully, a relative who was also a 'friend' of Michael's on this particular website, and who saw the offensive posts, contacted his parents immediately and explained to them what had been going on online.

Michael's parents knew they needed to take immediate action but became extremely frustrated when they could not easily find how permanently to remove Michael's profile and posts from the website. They eventually had to contact the social media website involved to have Michael's profile and details removed – and they could only do this because he was only 12 years old and most social websites do not allow children under 13 to have an account. If Michael had been a year older, the social media website in question may not have removed his account with only his parents' request – no matter what was being posted!

HOW TO PROTECT YOUR CHILD WHILE THEY ARE USING SOCIAL MEDIA

- It is recommended that you read the data privacy policy and terms and conditions/small print of the chosen social media website before allowing your child to create an account.

- Immediately after account creation, you should set/adjust the privacy settings before the child starts using the service or provides any further information.

- Ensure that your child never gives out personal information such as name, age or school details to anyone they do not know, and explain the reasons why.

- Ensure that your child chooses a screen name that cannot be easily linked to them.

- Ensure that your child knows not to upload photos without your permission and the reasons why.

- You should carry out a web search of your child's name at regular intervals to make sure that the privacy settings stay in effect and your child cannot be found by strangers online. This task can be automated easily by using browser tools such as Google Alerts, where the parent/carer can input the search specifications (i.e. their child's name) and the results will be emailed in a detailed report.

- You should report anyone who tries to contact or be 'friends' with your child to the relevant social media website if they are suspicious or have any doubts.

- You should also be aware that the police sometimes scan social media websites. Ensure that your child is aware of this also and explain that even a private posting mentioning or talking about doing something illegal can be found by the police.

REPORTING PROBLEMS

'Social reporting' is a relatively new way to report problems on many social media websites but can be very effective in stopping mean or bullying behaviour and parents/carers will be given the technical support of someone who can help them. Most social media websites these days will explain about social reporting and how to do so in their help section pages.

Remember that as a parent/carer you also have the option of reporting the incident to the relevant authorities or police. Remember to print out evidence if necessary to accompany your report.

SIMPLE SOCIAL MEDIA RULES TO TEACH YOUR CHILD

1. *Only have friends online that you know, like and trust in the real world.* Adjusting your child's privacy settings to 'friends only' on social media websites will restrict who sees their information, but you still need to teach your child only to have friends online that they know, like and trust in the real world and the reasons why. If someone is not their friend in the playground and in real life, there is no need for them to be 'friends' online.

2. *Make sure private information remains private.* Explain to your child that the less private information they supply when filling out a biography/profile the better, and also explain what can happen to their personal data if it ends up in wrong hands.

3. *Uncheck the 'public search results box'.* If you do not uncheck this box anyone can find your child's social media webpage through a browser search.

4. *Safeguard your reputation.* When your child posts something on a social media website it becomes available to anyone to read and is extremely hard to delete. What may seem humorous or contemporary today could be seen as offensive to other people tomorrow and ruin your child's reputation. Ensure that your child understands that they must think about the consequences before posting any comment and come to you if in any doubt.

WHAT ELSE CAN YOU DO?

1. Visit your country's government websites dedicated to child online safety. Most countries will have recognised websites where you can select videos for your child to watch regarding online safety. These

short films are usually from the child's point of view and can be quite shocking to the young child, so caution is advised, but you and your child will benefit from watching these videos.

2. Check with your child's school what their policy is with regard to social networking on either the school computers or mobile devices.

3. If your child is under 13 they are not legally permitted to join most social networking websites so you can contact the website involved and ask for your child's profile to be removed.

4. Check your child's 'browser history'. When your child visits a website it is saved in the browser history. You can easily and quickly view the websites your child has visited.

5. Install parental control software which will allow you to control your child's computer use and you can restrict access to social media websites if required.

6. Activate the 'safesearch' settings in your browser. Most browsers have settings now for parents to restrict access to various websites.

WHAT IS BLOGGING?

Blogs have been around for approximately ten years. The word 'blog' comes from 'Web log' and they are basically online diaries.

Anyone can set one up – that is the easy part! The difficult part is thinking of something interesting to say each time you 'blog'.

In simple terms, a blog is a website where you can write stuff about yourself on an ongoing basis. New information will appear at the top of the page so your visitors can read what's new and can comment on your post.

When blogging you can create your own personal page, write articles, upload photographs, meet new friends and communicate with them. You can add third-party pictures, articles and favourite pages to your blog.

Simple blogging rules to teach your child:

• Use good etiquette – keep language clean, do not be rude or mean or bully others.

• Respect the opinions of other commentators – opinions will differ.

• Don't use hyperlinks to websites in your posts/comments. Links can change over a period of time. Just because a website containing your favourite football club photograph is available now doesn't mean the link will take the visitor to that photograph later on.

- Stay safe and smart! Never give out personal information.

- Do not ask others for personal details such as email addresses or to meet them face to face.

WHAT ARE CHAT ROOMS?

Chat rooms are 'rooms' (pages on websites) where people around the world can meet and communicate with one another.

These are electronic chats and are real-time conversations. Typically, chat rooms are divided into different categories where people with similar interests can chat in one room (for example, Parents of Autistic Teenager Chat Room).

Chat room rules to teach your child:

- Always 'talk' politely and calmly and understand that what you mean to say may not always be clear in your typed text.

- Don't use abusive words or talk rudely to others. Most of the time the message your child sends can remain visible in this chat room for many years.

- Do not share any personal information with people you do not know in real life. This information can be used in the wrong way.

- Do not disclose your actual location, where you live or where you go to school.

- Choose a screen or nickname that has no relevance to you and does not reveal your real name or is sexually or violently suggestive.

- If someone is talking rudely or abusing you in a chat room, log out and tell an adult.

WHAT IS A FORUM?

An internet forum (or a message board, discussion group, bulletin board, web forum or virtual community as they are sometimes called) is basically the discussion area of a website (typically sorted into specific subjects) where members can create their own discussions or read and respond to posts by other forum members.

The rules for using a forum to teach your child are the same as they are for blogging and chat rooms.

WHAT IS INSTANT MESSAGING?

Instant messaging is a private chat service that anyone can use, as long as they have a valid email address. It is usually in the form of a small software package installed on your computer. Instant messaging (IM) is a type of online chat which offers real-time text transmission over the internet. Using email addresses you can search for and 'add' friends and then chat to them directly whenever they come online using this software.

Often this software offers the users the ability to do more than just text transmission chatting. Many models include the use of webcams in chat and even playing games against real-life opponents.

WHAT IS A WEBCAM AND IS IT SAFE TO USE?

A webcam – short for 'web camera' – is a digital camera that is connected to a computer or device. It can send live pictures to another location by means of the internet. Many desktop computer screens and laptops these days come with a built-in webcam and microphone, but these can also be added separately at any time and purchased inexpensively.

Webcams give other people an insight into your child's world so you need to be very careful when your child is using them.

Your child needs to be aware of the type of information that is visible in the room they are in (not just their bedroom) and remove anything that could make them vulnerable, such as names on certificates hanging on the wall or pieces of work from school that may have their name on.

Make sure your child knows to turn the webcam away from the room when it is not being used or is switched off. Criminals and dubious characters are always finding new ways of switching webcams on remotely, without you or your child's knowledge, so make your child aware of this fact.

Again, make sure you have installed good security software to remove any potential risks.

TASKS

1. Teach your child an example of how easy it is for someone online to lie. Create a fake social networking profile and upload pictures of your child so the profile claims to belong to them. Show this to your child and discuss how easy it was for you to pretend to be them and the dangers and risks that this could bring. Remember to *delete* the profile immediately after showing it as an example.

2. Teach your child what can happen to their photos if in the wrong hands. Take a photo of your child and use image-editing software to change the background of the photograph. Show this photo to your child and explain to them how easy it was for you to edit this and therefore how easy it would be for others to do.

CHAPTER 7

Mobile and Gaming Technology

WHAT IS MOBILE TECHNOLOGY?

> The smartphone is the second most popular internet-enabled device (51%), leapfrogging both games console (50%) and desktop computer ownership (41%) in the past year.
>
> (Ofcom 2013c, p.278)

Mobile technology is exactly what the name suggests – technology that is portable. Examples of mobile technology devices include:

- mobile phones and smartphones
- laptop and netbook computers
- palmtop computers or personal digital assistants
- global positioning system (GPS) devices
- wireless debit/credit card payment terminals.

As with computers, internet safety needs to be addressed for all these devices, because of the potential risks to your autistic child.

Mobile devices use a variety of communication technologies:

- wireless fidelity (wi-fi) – a type of wireless local area network technology
- Bluetooth – connects mobile devices wirelessly

- 'fourth/third generation' (4G/3G), global system for mobile communications (GSM) and general packet radio service (GPRS) data services – data networking services for mobile phones

- dial-up services – data networking services using modems and telephone lines

- virtual private networks – secure access to a private network.

Smartphones are basically mobile phones with internet access that are capable of a variety of additional functions such as social networking, listening to music, playing games, browsing the internet, checking emails, taking photos and watching videos or television.

It is strongly recommended that as a parent/carer you consider the following:

- Take the time to understand what your child's phone can do – all phones are different and you need to know what they are capable of so you can manage the risks.

- Set a PIN (Personal identification number) on your child's phone – setting a PIN is like setting a password. Remember that without a password other people can use the phone. This could mean that other people could access personal information stored on the device, create or access online accounts or even run up expensive bills.

- Set boundaries and monitor mobile phone usage. You should set rules about when and where the phone is used and for how long.

- Phones can be expensive so discuss this with your child and monitor costs. As well as the cost of calls, high bills can be run up when your child downloads apps, music or videos. Leaving data-roaming on when you go abroad will also run up huge bills so make sure this is turned off if going on holiday with your child. There are different ways to manage costs, such having a contract or a pay-as-you-go deal. Some phone companies also allow customers to use a credit limit system which sends you a text message when your limit is reached, although time and billing lags do not make this fail safe. Other companies can offer you a 'capped' contract, meaning that once your child has used up their monthly allowances you will be notified and the child will not be able to make further calls, or connect to the internet (unless you uncap the contract).

- Keep their mobile number private – your child needs to understand that their phone number should only be given to people they know and trust, so make sure that if they are concerned, they ask you first.

- Be prepared in case the phone is lost or stolen – know whom to contact to get the SIM card blocked. Every phone has a unique 'IMEI' number; make sure you write this down so that if the phone is stolen, the police can identify the phone if they find it. There is a sample Mobile Phone Information Form provided in Appendix 2 which will keep a record of all the important information and it is recommended that you use this.

THE BENEFITS OF MOBILE TECHNOLOGY FOR YOUR AUTISTIC CHILD

There are many benefits of using mobile technology:

- Your child has the facility to call emergency services.

- You can keep in constant contact with your child.

- You can track where your child is and where they have been.

- Your child's laptop or mobile phone can be used for schedules and as a source of reminders.

- Your child will always have something to do with their spare time.

HOW TO MONITOR YOUR CHILD'S MOBILE DEVICE

It is obviously more difficult to monitor your child's mobile device than it is to monitor their home computer, but you should take this just as seriously.

It is recommended that you download and install a mobile safety software package suitable for your child's phone. These mobile device software packages, which are widely available online, will:

- monitor your child's phone calls

- monitor text messages (SMS)

- record picture messages (MMS)

- track GPS locations

- mark contacts as 'allow' or 'alert'

- block web access

- set time blocking on the phone

- block new and existing applications on your child's phone, such as social networking apps (Facebook, Twitter, YouTube)
- block mobile games (*Angry Birds*, *Bejeweled*, etc.)
- block instant messaging apps (Yahoo Messenger, AIM, Beluga).

MOBILE PHONES AND SOCIAL MEDIA

A new feature available today on many social media mobile applications is the ability for people to check in when at a location. This is a modern way of telling people where you are or have been. When someone checks in using this application, the social media website will use the phone's geo-location features (including GPS and proximity to local wi-fi stations and cellular towers) to try to locate places near them or they have the option to type in their location manually.

While it could be fun for your child to share their location, it can also be dangerous if this information falls into the wrong hands. You need to teach your child to understand that this feature should be used with caution or not at all.

It is also possible to tag friends on social media websites who are with you at a place, so make sure your child is aware of this and that they ask friends not to tag them without their consent. It is possible to turn off the ability for friends to check your child into places, and it is recommended that you research and discuss this option with your child.

WHAT IS SEXTING?

Sexting is the sending of sexually explicit messages using mobile phones or instant messenger type applications. As technology has advanced and mobile phones now have the capability to record and send photos and videos, so has sending suggestive and explicit material to others increased, especially among teens.

Why is sexting a problem?

The ease with which photos and videos can be circulated and shared with others is the main concern. Any sexually explicit message or photo shared between two people has the potential to become a viral phenomenon if it falls into the wrong hands, so ensure that your child is aware of this fact.

What can parents do about sexting?

The best approach is to talk to your child about sexting. Ask them the following questions to get an understanding of their knowledge of sexting:

- Have you heard about sexting?

- Do you know what it is?

- Have you ever received a sexually explicit message?

- If so, do you know who it was from?

- Have you ever sent a sexually explicit message?

Discuss with them why they should be very careful before sending any sexually referenced texts or messages and the possible consequences of this action.

Common sexting slang

8	Oral Sex	GNRN	Get Naked Right Now
NIFOC	Naked In Front Of Computer	YWS	You Want Sex
		FMH	F*** Me Harder
143	I Love You	WYCM	Will You Call Me?
SorG	Straight Or Gay?	IWS	I Want Sex
cu46	See You For Sex	RU18	Are You 18?
JO	Jerk Off	Q2C	Quick To Come
DUM	Do You Masturbate?	CD9/	Parent/adult around
PAW	Parents Are Watching	Code9	
GNOC	Get Naked On Cam	RUH	Are You Horny?
PIR	Parent In Room	NALOPKT	Not A Lot Of People Know This
GYPO	Get Your Pants Off		
POS	Parent Over Shoulder	TDTM	Talk Dirty To Me

MOBILE TECHNOLOGY ADAPTED FOR THE AUTISTIC CHILD

A communicator

A communicator is an electronic device for supporting augmentative and alternative communication.

Communicators can show a structure of templates with images, similar to a communication board. Images can be pictograms, photos or drawings, which represent objects that the user can ask for, actions that can be carried out or things that the user wants to say (feelings or opinions, for instance). When an image is selected, an associated sound, previously stored, is often heard. This sound, which can be a word or a sentence, represents reinforcement for the user and allows people who listen to it to know what the user wants. Moreover, communicators provide links between templates. Visiting a new template is possible from a previous one, when a specific image is selected in it. This navigation between templates allows the construction of structured sentences, or the classification of actions and elements.

Communicators can also help to:

- decrease disruptive behaviours
- improve oral language
- solve communication issues
- reduce levels of anxiety
- increase the motivation to communicate.

Mobile support and learning

Children with autism are often taught how to express themselves by choosing one or more laminated picture flashcards and putting this message or sentence on a 'schedule'. There are now various software packages available to install on your child's mobile device which are similar to this teaching method and make schedule-keeping easier for you and your autistic child.

Learning 'games' (such as puzzles or memory games) are also available on mobile devices and these exercises can help your child to develop and enhance skills and abilities.

These types of games can help your child with:

- perception, visual and auditory discrimination
- vocabulary acquisition and comprehension of meaning
- memory development
- improving phonetics, syntax and pragmatics of language
- developing hand–eye co-ordination
- examining assumptions, conclusions and interpretations
- learning cause and effect.

Big button technology

Whether your child has vision or hearing problems, or has difficulties with motor co-ordination, there are plenty of 'big button' mobile phones currently available on the market.

Easy to operate, whether your child is text messaging or calling, a mobile with a big button keypad, plus a large text display and enhanced volume function, will ensure that your child is easily able to use the device properly.

Some other important features of big button technology are:

- dedicated quick dial buttons which you can assign numbers to

- an emergency call button. By holding the emergency button, the phone will automatically send a personalised text message to a previously agreed list of numbers. You can typically programme up to five emergency numbers.

- GPS tracking. Websites are now available which enable you to 'track' where your child is at any given time using their mobile device. You can also set virtual 'boundaries' on some of these websites and be alerted if your child crosses over these boundaries (for example, if you did not allow your child to go to the shops after school, you could set the shop as off-limits on the website. You would then be alerted if your child crossed over this boundary).

- hands-free speakerphone – so your child can use both hands while using the phone

- compatibility for use with hearing aids

- typically supplied with a desk stand for easy storage and charging.

GAMING TECHNOLOGY

According to Ofcom, 'nearly half of children aged 5–7 have a games console in their bedroom, rising to seven in ten 8–15 year olds' (Ofcom 2013a).

When we discuss 'gaming technology' in this book we refer to technology specifically designed for the user to play games. You need to know that as with all other modern technology devices that connect to the internet and/or the Web there are risks involved to the child and action is necessary to keep your child safe.

Remember that strangers can still approach and try to talk to your child via a games console connected to the internet.

Gaming consoles and parental controls

Consoles are capable of connecting to the internet via a home internet connection just like other computers. This allows users to download games or 'expansions' to existing games as well as playing online.

Most gaming consoles sold today have some parental control features or 'family settings' included which will control the types of games and films that children can play, view and/or download based on their content ratings. Many also provide settings to control the types of interaction carried out when the console is connected to the internet.

On purchase most of these consoles are automatically set to allow full access, so you are advised to change the settings to the appropriate rating for your child. It is strongly recommended that you read the instruction manual which comes with the console in order to familiarise yourself with the parental control settings.

Potential risks

Did you know that it is just as easy for your child to be at risk on a gaming console as they are on a computer? Children can still face potential risks such as contact with strangers and exposure to inappropriate material when using gaming consoles, and you need to act to protect your child in a similar way you would with any internet-enabled device.

Games consoles also have a high rate of addiction, so caution and time limits are recommended.

Also make sure that your child knows not to download and charge expensive games or extension packages to their credit/debit card if they have one – they could run up very large bills without realising why.

You should remember that internet safety advice is applicable to *all* internet-enabled devices.

What you can do to help your autistic child

CHECK THE AGE RATING OF GAMES

Just as with films, you should check the game's age rating before allowing your child to play any games.

Pan-European Game Information (PEGI) sets age ratings for games and classifies their content according to what is appropriate for different age groups and this helps you decide whether the game is suitable for your child.

There is also the Entertainment Software Rating Board (ESRB), which has an extremely useful website and ratings guidelines.

Remember, just because the game is rated suitable for a teenager, for example, it does not mean your autistic child is mentally ready for that game. If in doubt, research the game before purchase because refunds are hard to get.

PLAY THE GAMES YOURSELF

You should be aware of the content of the games your child plays and the different things they can do with them. The easiest way to find out about the games your child is playing is by joining in! Get your child to teach you how to play the game if needed and play alongside them for short periods of time to get a better understanding.

Playing the game with your child is a good way to open up a discussion and to get further information. You could ask your child some of these questions:

- Why do they like the game?
- What is so good about the game?
- Who do they talk to about the game or when directly playing the game?
- Who are their friends in the game?
- What offline friends play the same game?

To ensure safety it is important to stay up to date with new games and to ask your child regularly about the games they play and the people they are friends with.

Teach your child what is acceptable behaviour

Children can be very mean to each other online so it is very important that you educate your child in 'netiquette' – manners expected when online – and ensure that your child knows to be nice to other people while playing games online, and to behave just as they would in the playground.

CHAPTER 8

Computer Hacking and Autism

WHAT IS A COMPUTER HACKER?

In simple terms, a computer hacker is someone who has the knowledge and skills to use technology to get inside a network and/or computer(s) without the owner's knowledge either to gather personal information such as bank details or passwords, or to do damage to the system.

There are three main different types of hackers:

1. *Black hat hackers.* These are the 'bad guys'. A black hat hacker will use his skills to disrupt computer systems, usually for maliciousness or personal gain.

2. *White hat hackers.* The 'good guys'! The white hat hacker term belongs to computer security experts who specialise in testing and development to ensure the security of an organisation's systems (normally their employer).

3. *Grey hat hackers.* This term is typically used to identify someone who falls between a white or black hat hacker.

ORIGINS OF HACKING

In the 1950s and 1960s engineers from the Massachusetts Institute of Technology in the USA established the term 'hacking'. These initial so-called 'hacks' were only innocent technical projects/experiments and were used as learning tools. Later, however, other programmers began attaching the general term to less moral activities and the expression sprouted.

As both computer networking and the internet grow, so do the numbers of hackers attempting to find weaknesses to exploit vulnerable systems for their own purposes.

HACKING VS. CRACKING

Some computer programmers argue that someone breaking into a secure network is better called a 'cracker', but most people misuse the saying 'hacking' instead and know this word as the general term. A malicious and deliberate attack on a computer network is technically known as 'cracking', while activities having good intentions are known as 'hacking'.

COMMON NETWORK HACKING/ CRACKING TECHNIQUES

Cracking on computer networks is often done using small scripts, software or network programs. These programs typically manipulate the data passing through a network, often catching keyboard strokes or personal details.

Cracking techniques on networks include creating worms, initiating denial-of-service (DoS) attacks or unauthorised remote access connections.

AUTISM AND HACKING/CRACKING – WHY THE MEDIA ATTENTION?

Becoming a 'hacker' or 'cracker' is exceptionally challenging, as it takes a lot of time and determination to understand and comprehend the sophisticated complex processes needed to break and enter a network. For the average PC user it is an impossible task. For the highly computer literate autistic person, it can seem simple to do.

Hacking or cracking, whatever term you prefer, is now thankfully a criminal offence in most countries, but recently autism has been used as a defence in some hacking cases and this has caused media exposure and ongoing debates.

WHY COULD AUTISM BE USED AS A DEFENCE AGAINST HACKING/CRACKING?

Because of the challenges of autism, such as obsessive behaviour and poor social skills, computers are an ideal environment for the autistic person to sit happily for hours working on an obsession, such as obtaining information from secure sources, for example, government websites, or trying to break passwords.

However, because the autistic child is often extremely naïve, especially when it comes to social cues and communication skills, they are unable to determine right from wrong and therefore the debate is currently ongoing as to whether autism can be used as a defence. If you do not know that something is wrong how can you be punished for it?

A recent example of this is a UK citizen with Asperger syndrome who was arrested after being caught attempting to break into NASA (National Aeronautics and Space Administration) and Pentagon networks in the USA. He faced extradition to the USA to stand charges (which were later withdrawn by the UK Home Secretary), and he has used his condition as a defence against his alleged crimes.

The young man in question states that he was only seeking the information for the good of humanity and not for criminal purposes, claiming he had become so obsessed with finding the information that he lost sight of reality and the consequences of his actions.

The real legal question ongoing at the moment is, 'Do people on the autism spectrum know right from wrong when it comes to computer use, or does their condition make them so determined and so "addicted" to the task at hand that they are unable to stop?'

Talented autistic computer users will often begin to look for ways to exhibit their skills online to programmers of similar talents – and if your autistic child is gifted they will easily find an appreciative audience on hacking websites to show off to. Remember that your child can also feel peer pressure from people online to become involved in hacking.

Also, because of their lack of social skills, autistic children may have no idea how to react when contacted by a 'hacker' (usually the hacker will approach your child online in a social and friendly way, as paedophiles do using social media websites). It will be the aim of the 'hacker' to discover how talented your child is with computers and to see if they can use your child's skills to create and develop hacking tools and programs.

However, you should not worry. It is only a minority of children who go on to become crackers, and experts actually believe that this is a valuable opportunity for companies and organisations in the computer industry to employ people on the autism spectrum and put their amazing talents to beneficial use.

If your autistic child is exceptionally gifted with computers you should encourage this, but make sure they are always in a safe environment and not breaking any laws and potentially growing into tomorrow's cracker.

DANGER SIGNS TO WATCH OUT FOR

Is your child obsessed with computers and programming?

If your child is obsessed with computers and programming it is extremely important that you know what your child is doing online at all times to avoid them becoming groomed to be a hacker/cracker.

Has your child asked for a new computer?

As technology advances, so does the need for hackers/crackers to have the latest and fastest computers. If your child has asked for a new computer, check the reason behind the request and make sure it is not for hacking/cracking purposes.

Are there any unrecognisable programs installed on your child's computer?

Because most hackers/crackers use software that is either ready-made or bespoke to break into networks, it is a good idea for you to ensure that you know and recognise what programs are installed on your child's computer. If there are any software programs installed that are unfamiliar it is recommended that you research each program name online to determine what it is for exactly, and to uninstall it if warranted.

Has your child asked to switch ISPs?

Your ISP (internet service provider) is exactly what the name suggests – the company that provides your internet connection. This can be broadband or dial-up.

The most common ISPs have already stepped in with sophisticated blocking technology and will prevent your child accessing some hacking websites – but not all.

The smaller ISPs still have no defence against this and this is well known by hackers/crackers. If your child requests a change in ISP it could be for no other reason than to enable them to hack/crack more easily.

Has your child asked to change operating systems?

Apple Mac or Windows are the most common operating systems for standard home computers today. If your child asks to use another operating system on their computer such as Linux, which is the preferred operating system of hackers/crackers, you should beware. Although Linux is a very popular operating software package and used extensively throughout the world, it is generally aimed towards the more able computer user – not something a child would normally insist on. So although it is not illegal software, this could be a red flag that your child is attempting cracking/hacking techniques and it is recommended that the request is denied unless a full explanation and reasons are given which the parent/carer understands.

Have you found any hacking manuals/books or printouts in your home?

If your child has an interest in hacking/cracking it is possible that they may have manuals or instructions in books/printouts and may leave them around the house. If you find even one of these manuals, do not dismiss it as only curiosity – take steps to ensure that your child is not training to become a hacker/cracker of tomorrow.

ORGANISATIONS TO WATCH OUT FOR

Autistic children may find, be approached by and/or join 'hacker' groups and organisations, and you need to be fully aware of these to keep your child at a distance and therefore safe.

Anonymous

Originating in 2003 on the online forum '4chan', Anonymous (used as a mass noun) in very simple terms is a wide-spread association, or group, of 'hacktivists'. A hacktivist (a combination of hacker and activist) is someone who uses computers and/or the internet to broadcast and/or circulate political views and opinions. Typically, members participate in protests (online and offline) in retribution against anti-digital piracy rulings. Anonymous, however, has recently become infamous for carrying out various distribution of denial-of-service (DDoS) attacks on government, religious and corporate websites.

Figure 8.1 Beware of Anonymous and other hacking organisations

Anonymous members (known as 'Anons') can be easily recognised because they often wear contemporary Guy Fawkes masks (see Figure 8.1).

In 2012, *Time* magazine called Anonymous one of the '100 most influential "people" in the world'.

You are advised to prohibit your child from having any association with groups like these. There is just no benefit to your child in becoming a member of such a group.

LulzSec

A small group of 'Anons' joined forces and founded the hacker group Lulz Security, commonly abbreviated to LulzSec, in 2011. This group has carried out many and frequent attacks against individuals and organisations in the few years since it began, the majority of damage accomplished using distributed denial-of-service attacks.

AntiSec

The Anti Security Movement (also written as Antisec and Anti-sec) is a movement opposed to the computer security industry, and in 2011 hackers from both Anonymous and LulzSec collaborated on a series of cyber-attacks known as 'Operation AntiSec'.

TASK

To get a better understanding of your child's knowledge of hacking and to promote discussion, consider asking your child the following questions:

- Do you know what hacking is?
- Do you know the difference between cracking and hacking?
- Do you know that hacking/cracking is illegal?
- Have you heard of Linux or any other operating system apart from Windows or Mac?
- Do you know of any hacking/cracking software programs?
- Have you heard of the group Anonymous?
- Have you ever seen someone wearing the Guy Fawkes mask and did you know what it meant?
- Have you ever been approached to program a script or virus?

You should remember that it is only a small minority of autistic children who have the talent and the advanced capabilities needed to hack/crack networks. Do not allow this potential danger to interfere with your child's computer use – make sure the child is aware of the risks, knows right from wrong and understands that cracking is illegal.

Find out how many hours your child spends using a computer by completing the Child's Computer Log – Hours Per Week in Appendix 2.

CHAPTER 9

Digispeak Dictionary

Understanding Online Abbreviations

INTRODUCTION

Internet slang originated in the early days of the internet and is used in social networking, chat rooms, online gaming, mobile phone texting, and so on.

Acronyms are used as a form of shorthand for phrases frequently used during online communications or chats.

This new language has been given various titles including 'digispeak', 'textspeak', 'geekspeak', 'Internet speak', 'Webspeak' and 'IMglish' and below is a list of the most common phrases adapted in this way.

THE DIGISPEAK DICTIONARY

AFAIK	As far as I know	CAP	Cover all possibilities
AFAIR	As far as I remember	CSN	Computer says no
AFK	Away from keyboard	CTA	Call to action
AOB	Any other business	CU	See you
A/S/L	Age, sex, location	CUL	See you later
ATM	At the moment		
AYT	Are you there	DETI	Don't even think it
		DQMOT	Don't quote me on
BBL	Be back later		this
BFF	Best friend forever	EOD	End of day
BFN	Bye for now		
BRB	Be right back	F2F	Face to face
BTDT	Been there, done that	FFS	For f***'s sake
BTW	By the way	FOAF	Friend of a friend
		FWD	Forward

FWIW	For what it's worth	OIC	Oh, I see
FYI	For your information	OMG	Oh my gosh/God!
		OTOH	On the other hand
GAL	Get a life	OTP	On the phone
GD&R	Grinning, ducking and running		
		PAL	Parents are listening
GMTA	Great minds think alike	PIR	Parents in room
		PITA	Pain in the ass
GR8	Great	PMJI	Pardon my jumping in
GSOH	Good sense of humour	POV	Point of view
		PRW	Parents are watching
HB	Hurry back	RL	Real life
HHOK	Ha, ha, only kidding	ROFL	Rolling on the floor laughing
IAW	In accordance with	ROFLMAO	ROFL my ass off
IDK	I don't know		
IMCO	In my considered opinion	SIT	Stay in touch
		SLAP	Sounds like a plan
IMHO	In my humble opinion	SMS	Short messaging service
IMO	In my opinion		
IOW	In other words	STFU	Shut the f*** up!
		SUP	What's up?
JIT	Just in time		
JK	Just kidding	TB	Text back
JOOTT	Just one of those things	TBH	To be honest
		THX	Thanks
		TIA	Thanks in advance
KK	Okay, all right	TMI	Too much information
KPC	Keeping parents clueless	TMTH	Too much to handle
		TTFN	Ta, ta for now (goodbye)
LMAO	Laughing my ass off		
LOL	Laugh out loud	TTT	Thought that too
LMIRL	Let's meet in real life	TTYL	Talk to you later
LULZ	Lots of laughs	TTYS	Talk to you soon
LYLAS	Love ya like a sister	TU	Thank you
		TY	Thank you
MYOB	Mind your own business	U2U	Up to you
MWA	A kiss (the sound of 'mwa')	WB	Write back
		WFM	Works for me
N2M	Not too much	WIIFM	What's in it for me?
NALOPKT	Not a lot of people know that	WIP	Work in progress
		WTF	What the f***?
		WYP	What's your problem?

XOXO	Hugs and kisses
YOLO	You only live once
YOYO	You're on your own
YT	You there?

CHAPTER 10

Adapting Your Child's Workstation Area

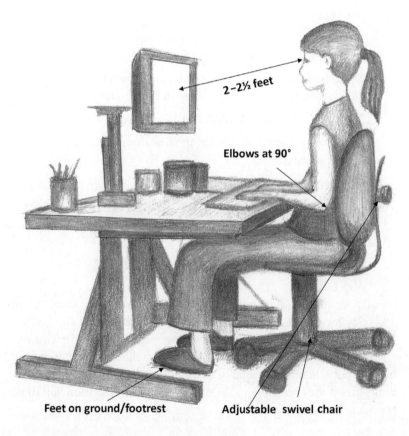

Figure 10.1 Recommended workstation area

INTRODUCTION

It is extremely important for you to provide your autistic child with not only a safe environment when using computers, but a *healthy* one! As modern technology continues to grow into a bigger part of your child's life, the necessity to be aware and pay attention to computer-related health issues also increases as there is the potential for problems to develop over time.

To take steps to prevent computer-related health issues, you should ensure that when your autistic child uses a computer either at home or at school the workstation area is adapted appropriately for your child.

IMPORTANT THINGS TO TEACH YOUR CHILD

You need to teach your autistic child some simple yet very important health and safety rules:

- *Do not* sit too close to the monitor and turn away from the monitor frequently (this helps prevent strained vision).

- *Do* take frequent rest breaks (moving away from the computer helps circulation and rests both the eyes and the body).

- *Do* stand up and stretch often (this also helps circulation).

- *Do* blink frequently (this helps prevent dry eyes caused by staring at the monitor).

- *Avoid using* the mouse for long periods of time (which can cause Carpal Tunnel Syndrome).

- *Sit upright and do not slouch* (this can help with posture and prevent neck and/or back problems).

SENSORY ISSUES

We all have and use seven senses: sight, sound, touch, taste, smell, balance and body awareness. Autism can affect all these senses and children who have problems in this area can be either oversensitive or undersensitive.

You should ensure that your child's workstation is not only safe and healthy but tailored individually to your autistic child's sensory issues/ difficulties if they are present. When setting up a workstation you should consider the following areas.

Sight (visual system)

If your autistic child is oversensitive to light it is recommended that you always ensure that the room where the workstation is located is bright – but not overly bright (i.e. do not use fluorescent lighting). Try reducing light-bulb wattage. Make sure that there is no reflective glare from a window and adjust blinds/curtains accordingly. If this is still a concern, consider allowing the child to wear sunglasses.

If your child is undersensitive, consider using additional visual supports such as coloured pictures or photographs.

Sound (auditory system)

Ensure that the workstation is placed in a quiet area, away from any noise, and that doors and windows are shut to avoid external and potentially distracting sounds.

If the child has speakers connected to the computer, ensure that these are set at a level suitable for your child. Remember that when a computer starts up the software makes a sound – make sure the speaker volume is not set too loud in case this frightens your child.

If the workstation the autistic child uses is utilised by others, such as members of the family, try to make sure there are no telephones (mobile or landline) on the workstation area – if they ring they could cause much distraction to your autistic child.

If your child continues to exhibit signs of noise distraction, consider allowing them to wear headphones or ear plugs.

Touch (tactile or somatosensory system)

Your autistic child will have to use the sense 'touch' when using a computer. If they have difficulties in this area, for example if they do not like touching a keyboard or mouse, consider using touch-screen technology to make it easier for the child.

You should remember that computers generate heat. Ideally your child's computer should be positioned in a well-ventilated room. Consider using fans or air conditioning in the room if required.

Smell (olfactory system)

Avoid using strong-smelling chemicals when cleaning your child's workstation area and remember that your autistic child may be oversensitive to smell. Remove any unwanted or strong smells to avoid distraction by airing the room out thoroughly and regularly. Do not use air fresheners in the room or allow strong smelling foods.

Remember that even if you do not smell the chemical cleaning product, your autistic child, if they are oversensitive to smell, could still be affected by it.

Balance (vestibular system)
Make sure your autistic child is sitting in a comfortable chair, suitable for their size, with their feet firmly on the ground. A good quality chair that has hand rests, and therefore something to hold on to, can help with their balance difficulties.

Body awareness (proprioception system)
It is possible that your autistic child may not know their own strength, or have little body awareness, so you should make sure that the computer is set up with nothing visibly 'sticking out' of it (such as a USB[1] device) which can be pulled, knocked and/or easily broken.

Try keeping unrelated items off the workstation area, such as stationery, which can be easily knocked over or damaged and causes distraction.

You should also consider using coloured tape to set boundaries on the workstation desk/floor; for example, if you do not want the child to touch the printer put red tape on the desk in front of the relevant device and make sure the child knows not to cross this 'boundary'.

RECOMMENDED GUIDELINES
It is recommended that you always use safe and adjustable furniture that is tailored to the size of the child and take into consideration the need to adapt the workstation as the child grows. The correct posture while using a computer is one that offers comfort and circulation to the back, arms, legs and neck.

Viewing distance/monitor position
It is recommended that your child's screen/monitor should be approximately two to two and a half feet away from their eyes and the screen should be easy to read at that distance (use a larger screen font size if needed).

---

1   Universal Serial Bus.

Remember to position monitors so that glare and reflections are avoided.

Seat height and position

Ideally your child needs to look slightly down when looking at the screen/monitor, so it is recommended that you adjust the seat height so that the top of the screen/monitor is approximately at the child's forehead height.

Although adjustable seating is highly recommended, if you are unable to provide this for your child, correct positioning can still be achieved by using cushions to lift the child higher if required.

Ideally the chair you provide for your child should swivel as this will make movement while using the computer easier for your child.

Arm position

When typing or using the keyboard, the child's arms should be able to rest comfortably at 90° angles.

Feet position

If your child's feet are dangling while using the computer it is possible that it will be cutting off circulation to the legs, so ideally your child's chair should be adjusted so that their feet can sit flat on the ground. If this is not possible, it is recommended that your child use a footrest. If you cannot provide a footrest, consider using large books stacked high enough so the child can rest their feet comfortably.

Mouse/pointing device

It is wise to remember that most standard mice purchased are built to fit adult hands. It is recommended that you provide your child with a mouse tailored to the size of your child's hand.

For children who do not have the developed motor skills needed to use a mouse, touchpads and rollerballs are available which are typically easier to manipulate and may be more suitable. You should also consider the size of the child's hand when purchasing such equipment.

Keyboards

As with mice, you should take into consideration the size of the child's hands and the ease with which the child can use the keyboard.

There are smaller, child-size keyboards available to purchase separately or if you are considering buying a system for your child, notebooks have smaller keyboards and therefore may be more suitable for your autistic child.

'Alternative' keyboards are also available to purchase. These change the standard 'qwerty' keyboard to suit typists of different skills – for example, there is one available for a typist who uses the right hand only when typing. These keyboards may help those autistic children who have difficulties with fine motor skills or have limited dexterity.

You should also consider using on-screen keyboards if this method suits their child better. Most operating systems these days provide the option for an on-screen keyboard.

It is recommended that you take the time to shop around for a keyboard most suitable for your child.

Touch screens

A touch-screen monitor gives the user control of the computer simply by touching the screen. No mouse or keyboard is needed. Some autistic children have difficulties understanding that the mouse controls movement on the screen, so if this is the case with your child you should consider this option. This is also a good option for autistic children who struggle with a conventional mouse and keyboard because it will reduce frustration for the child and help make their computer experience more enjoyable.

Just with typical monitors or screens, touch-screen monitors should be positioned so that glare and reflections are avoided.

Environment

You should remember that electrical appliances can be dangerous, so caution is highly recommended. Ensure that your child understands not to eat or drink while using their computer, and explain the possible consequences (e.g. fire, damaged equipment).

If possible, arrange to get electrical appliances checked regularly by a reputable and trusted source. Also ensure that sockets or extension cables are not overloaded.

Cables

Ensure that the area where your child's computer is located is free from exposed cables which they could potentially trip on or damage.

USB devices/Wireless adapters

Remember that devices (such as a mouse) which are connected to the computer can be pulled and the cable easily damaged. Wireless devices should be considered if this is the case with your child. It will not stop the child throwing the device, but if they do at least the cable will not be ripped out of the system.

Some USB devices/adapters are designed in such a way that they can 'stick out' of the system (such as wireless adapters or memory sticks). If you leave anything sticking out of a computer it is vulnerable to being knocked or kicked and could be damaged. Ensure that you keep USB devices out of reach unless in use and consider USB extension cables for such devices.

IDEAL WORKSTATION SETTINGS

It is recommended that you do a complete workstation assessment to ensure that the area is arranged suitably for your autistic child, as this can help the workstation continue to remain set up correctly for future use – especially if others use it.

Information to consider in this assessment could include ideal speaker volume settings, chair height setting, and so on. This information can then be held near the computer – and/or made available to the school – so that all those who support the autistic child will know what the ideal settings are.

There is a Workstation Settings Form for you to use in Appendix 2 of this book.

A–Z of Internet Terminology

Note from the author: This list could potentially be never-ending, as you can imagine, so I have kept it very simple using only the most common terminology currently used relevant to the internet.

Anti-virus software – A software program designed to detect and remove computer viruses. There are many commercial software companies online offering either free-of-charge or purchasing options for this type of software and it is highly recommended that you install this on their child's computer. Without this your child and computer security are at risk.

Applet – A small Java program which runs in the background of a website and allows the option for webmasters to have animation, calculators, sound effects or other interactive functions available on their website. (See also 'Java'.)

Bandwidth – The rate at which data or information travels through a network connection. Bandwidth is usually measured in bits per second. A kilobit is a thousand bits per second. These days we often see this measured at megabits (million bits) per second.

Bit – A 'bit' (taken from the term 'binary digit') is the name given to the smallest element of computer data, or in simple terms the smallest unit of information (memory) on a computer. (See also 'Byte'.)

Blog – The word 'blog' comes from 'Web log'. Blogs are basically online diaries.

Bookmark – Browsers these days typically have the ability for users to save (bookmark) to a favourite websites file so that they can be easily available for future use.

Broadband – A high bandwidth connection to the internet. Broadband is available over phone lines (see 'ISP'), or via cable or satellite connections.

Browser – A software program essential to modern-day computers as this is the software needed to view and search the internet. Microsoft Internet

Explorer or Google Chrome are trusted examples of popular browsers today.

Browser hijacker – A very inconvenient common spyware program that will automatically change your browser's home page settings and can be a troublesome problem to remove. If your child downloads from untrusted sources there is a good chance their computer will become affected by this type of threat. A 'spyware removal' program (which differs from an anti-virus program but may be included in your anti-virus package) is often required to stop this attack permanently.

Bulletin board – An area of a website where users can post messages for other users to read and respond to. Readers also have the option to contact the author of a bulletin board message by email. (See also 'Discussion group'.)

Byte – A byte typically represents one character, such as 'A', in a computer memory, and is made up of eight bits. (See also 'Bit'.)

Cache – When you or your child use a browser to search the internet, a file is automatically created on the hard drive which saves information such as addresses, text and graphics from recently visited websites. If you revisit the website, the computer will find the relevant information from the cache file often without the need to download the information from the internet again, making it easier and faster for the user to view the websites.

Chat – A feature offered by some websites that will allow users to chat to each other by typing messages which are displayed almost instantly on the screens of other users who are using the same chat room. The number of users using the same chat service can vary hugely, normally depending on the chat topic of conversation. Usually users remain anonymous, using nicknames or pseudonyms to identify themselves.

Chat room – A specific webpage (room) of a website where users can 'chat' with each other by typing messages. Chat room conversations are typically organised into specific subject topics.

Cookie – The term given when your browser saves information and transmits this back to the website's server. Cookies are designed to be a harmless and time-saving way to use a website and may include information from previous website visits or registration details, such as your login details or user preferences. Often the website server may use the information stored in the cookie to tailor the display it sends to the user, or it may keep track of the different pages within the site that the user has browsed or accessed.

Cracker – Someone with the technical knowledge and skills needed to break into computer networks using the internet normally for personal gain or to cause harm. (See also 'Hacker'.)

Default – If you set a program or device as a 'default' you are basically telling your computer to select that option at all times until you specify another setting. For example, you could set your default email program to Outlook and unless you change this in the main settings, all emails will open with Outlook.

Disclosure – Companies and/or websites who offer your personal information to third parties, for example marketing lists, must make available to readers a full disclosure policy document.

Discussion group – Typically, discussion group members can read and post comments about a specific topic. (See also 'Bulletin Boards'.)

Domain name – The address used for a website. All websites need to have a domain name and this name can be anything (but owners will logically try to find a name suitable for their company). (See also 'URL'.)

A website address also includes a suffix at the end such as .com, .org, .gov or .edu. Typically, the suffix will indicate what type of organisation the website is. For example:

.com – the best known domain suffix, which originally stood for 'commercial', to indicate a website that could be used for private, commercial purposes only but is today used for many top-level websites.

.co.uk – this suffix is typically associated with UK company/business websites.

.net – originally intended for websites directly related to the internet only, but is now used for a wide variety of sites.

.edu – typically used for educational institutions such as schools and universities only.

.ac.uk – typically used for UK academic websites.

.org – originally intended for non-commercial and/or non-profit organisations such as charities but is also used for a wide variety of websites today.

.gov – typically used for government websites only.

DDoS (DoS) – This is a term used to describe denial-of-service or *distributed* denial-of-service attacks (DDoS/DoS attack) and is used typically by crackers in an attempt to damage networks and/or gather personal information.

Download(ing) – When you transfer (copy) information or files from a website or other Web service to your computer or device you are downloading that information. (See also 'Upload'.)

DSL (Digital Subscriber Line) – This is a term given to accessing the internet at very high speeds using standard phone lines.

Email (Electronic Mail) – An email is the modern-day letter. However, these letters (or messages) are sent using a computer and through a network rather than via the postal service. Email addresses always include the '@' symbol, such as joebloggs@autism.co.uk. Though emails are usually made up of text, the capacity to attach files that include graphics, sound and video is available.

Encryption – This is a technological way of making messages or data unreadable to everyone except those authorised and is typically password-protected information. Encryption methods are often employed when debit/credit cards are used during online shopping transactions or in extremely sensitive email messaging.

Ethernet – The most common way to connect computers together and/or to a network. Ethernet cables are used to connect a computer to another computer, or a computer to a network device.

End user licensing agreement – Information to which the computer user is referred in the context of downloading software. The 'end user' is the person for whom software is ultimately designed.

Executable file – A file that is created in such a way it can be directly executed (open/run) by the computer without the need for any other software (data or information files typically need additional software to open/edit, whereas executable files do not). Unless from a trusted and responsible source it is inadvisable to open any executable files as they can contain spyware or even viruses.

FAQ (Frequently Asked Questions) – Many websites will offer a section which lists and answers the most popular or most asked questions about that specific website. The FAQ page often provides useful information for a new user and can be a valuable resource for parents/carers researching age-appropriate websites for their child.

File sharing – The accessing of files on one computer from another computer.

Firewall – Any hardware or software that secures files on your computer by blocking unapproved or unknown access on your network.

Flaming – Posting or sending a deliberately confrontational or offensive message to someone specific or various people via a discussion board, newsgroup or email.

FTP (File Transfer Protocol) – A way of transferring data and files using the internet from one computer to another.

Gateway – If the exchange of information is required across two or more compatible networks, a gateway is used to translate between the protocols.

Hacker – Someone with the technical knowledge and skills needed to break into computer networks using the internet. (See also 'Cracker'.)

Hardware – The machines, wiring and other physical mechanical components that make up a computer system, such as the central processing unit, monitor, keyboard and mouse, as well as other equipment such as printers and speakers.

Home page – This is typically the first page of a website and will normally include an introduction to the website and/or company and provide the user with the means of navigation through the website. Also, every 'browser' program will allow users to set the first (home) page they view when the software program starts up.

HTML (Hypertext Markup Language) – The most common language used for creating hypertext websites or documents.

HTTP (Hypertext Transfer Protocol) – The most common language used to enable computers connected to the Web to communicate with each other.

Hyperlink – Basically an image or selection of text on a webpage which users can click and it will take them (link them) to another page, document or file in that website. Text links on websites are usually underlined, and images often have borders around them. If a user hovers the mouse over the link, the arrow cursor on the screen will normally turn to a pointed hand. (See also 'Links'.)

IM or **Instant Message** – Instant messaging services are typically small software programs which enable users to chat to other users in real-time conversations. Anyone can use these often free-of-charge programs as only an email address is needed to register and download/install the software.

Internet – The global connection of computer networks which work on a common addressing system. The internet is also sometimes referred to as the 'net'.

Intranet – This is the private network of a company or organisation and uses technology similar to the internet, but is for confidential and/or internal use only, and is not available to the public. Companies use intranets to manage projects, organise diaries/schedules, distribute data and share information, and so on.

IP (Internet Protocol) – The computer language that allows computer programs to communicate over the internet.

IP address (or IP number) – When your computer connects to a network a set of four numbers, each between 0 and 255, separated by full stops (e.g. 192.168.1.2) is given to your computer and this unique number identifies your computer on the network.

IRCs (Internet Relay Chats) – IRCs were the earliest form of online chatting. IRCs are typically a protocol and a program that allow users to 'chat' online live on a website. These IRCs usually centre around a common interest.

ISDN (Integrated Services Digital Network) – A method of connecting to the internet over standard phone lines at speeds higher than a standard 56 kilobit modem typically allows.

ISP (Internet Service Provider) – A company which provides its customers with access to the internet using phone lines, cabling or satellites.

Java – A computer programming language invented by Sun Microsystems. Using Java, Web developers can create small programs called 'applets' that allow websites to include animations, calculators, scrolling text, sound effects and games. (See also 'Applet'.)

Keystroke logger – A hardware device or (more typically) a software program that records each keystroke made on a particular computer keyboard. Keystroke loggers can be used by parents/carers in an effort to find out what their child is doing while using the computer if other methods fail.

Keyword/Keyphrase – When you want to search the internet for something you are required to input a keyword or phrase to help the browser search for and find the most appropriate matches to your search.

LAN (Local Area Network) – A network of computers that are generally positioned near each other in the home or small office and are connected by ethernet cables and/or to a router.

Link – The name given to a word, phrase or image highlighted in a hypertext document which when clicked will navigate to other related information on that website. Links may be indicated by underlining, a colour contrast or a border.

Machine Access Code (MAC address) – The unique number by which every computer is identified.

Modem – A hardware device that allows computers to communicate with the internet (characteristically called 'dial-up' access) by transmitting and receiving data over a telephone line. Modems come in different speeds. The higher the speed, the faster the data is transmitted/received. Because the fastest widely available modems are only capable of transmitting data at 56 kilobits per second, they are not often used today. Broadband has helped in the extinction of the modem. (See 'Broadband'.)

Monitoring software – Software programs that allow a parent/carer to monitor or track the websites or email messages that a child visits or reads, without necessarily blocking access.

Multimedia – Information presented in more than one format, such as text, audio, video, graphics and images.

Navigation – Most websites will have a method visitors can use to find their way easily through the website and this can be delivered either in text or image form.

Navigation and Click-stream data – Data or information users generate when browsing the internet. It can often include information regarding the links on which a user clicks, pages a user visits and the amount of time spent on each page. Most websites will use this information when compiling website statistic reports.

Net – Shortened name for the internet.

Netiquette – The informal rules and manners/courtesy expected of people when using the internet.

Newsgroups – Discussion groups on the internet (not on the Web, which is only one area of the internet). Newsgroups are classified by subjects and do not necessarily deal just with 'news'. Participants in a newsgroup can hold discussions by posting messages for others to read and by responding to the messages posted by others.

Online contact information – Information that allows someone to be contacted or located on the internet, such as an email address or website.

Operating system – The principal software program that controls and runs your computer. Major operating systems today include Windows, Mac OS and Linux.

Phishing – An identity theft scam which is very common. Criminals will send out messages or emails that impersonate correspondence from trusted and legitimate websites. The fake messages generally link to websites which are also counterfeit. On these fake websites, victims are instructed to enter personal information for authentication or confirmation purposes. The information, when submitted, does not go to the trusted company, however – it goes straight to the thieves!

Plug-in – A small software program update that enriches a larger piece of software by adding features or functions.

Pop-up advertisements (or pop-ups) – Unsolicited advertising that appears in its own browser window. Most browsers these days have pop-up blocking software included in the installation process.

Posting – When you send a message to a discussion group or other public message area on the internet you are 'posting' that message. The message itself is called a 'post'.

Privacy policy – The policy under which the company or organisation operating a website handles the personal information collected about visitors to the site. Many websites publish their privacy policy on their website for users to inspect. The policy usually includes a description of the personal information which is collected by the site, how the information will be used, with whom it will be shared, and whether the visitors have the option to exercise control over how their information will be used.

Profile – A page dedicated to an individual on a website which can display information about that person, including their contact details, photos/videos, a description, interests, and so on.

Search engine – A software program used for the retrieval of data, files or documents from a database, network or the internet. This tool enables users to find information quickly. Search engines use keywords or keyphrases to find websites which match the required information.

Server – A computer connected to a network of other computers, used as the main system or more specifically to provide (serve up) data to the other computers connected to that network. A server is also typically used to back up/store data and control user permissions. A Web server transmits websites over the internet when it receives a Web browser's request for a page. A server can also be called a 'host' or a 'node'.

Social media – The term to describe websites and online software/tools which enable people to interact with each other – by sharing information, opinions, knowledge and interests.

Software – A computer program created to contain the data and instructions needed to enable computer hardware to operate successfully. Operating system software, such as Windows or Mac OS, runs the computer while software which provides a more particular purpose, such as word processing programs and anti-virus programs, is called applications software.

Spam – Any unsolicited junk emails sent out to a large number of people to promote products or services. 'Porn spam' is typically sexually explicit unsolicited emails referring to inappropriate promotional or commercial websites.

Spider – A software program that 'crawls' the Web, searching and indexing websites to create a database that can be easily searched by a search engine. These spiders are used by some of the largest search engines today. If you are a webmaster, you want spiders to crawl your website as this will enhance the listing for your website on the search engine.

Subscription data – The information that you provide to an online service or website when you sign up to become a member. Subscription data usually includes your name, address, email address, telephone number, and so on.

Surf – When someone searches for information on the internet or Web.

TCP/IP (Transmission Control Protocol/Internet Protocol) – The protocol, or method, that computers use to communicate with each other over the internet.

Time-limiting software – A software program that allows users to set time limits for access to the internet, computer games, or other software programs. Recommended for parents/carers of autistic children.

Trojans – These are usually small programs created specifically to allow third parties unauthorised access to your computer. Trojans are often used these days to manipulate a computer into sending out unsolicited emails to all contacts on that computer.

Troll – A 'troll' is a relatively new term and is internet slang for someone who posts (typically anonymously) disagreeable or defamatory/offensive comments online either to start arguments or to hurt/embarrass another person or organisation.

Uninstall – When you uninstall a software program you are removing that program from a computer. This is normally done using the Control Panel. Often software, especially untrusted and downloaded software, is extremely hard to remove from your computer and the standard option may not be enough, so you may have to remove these with a separate uninstall program. These additional programs will remove all files that were installed with the program and also restore any adjustments made to system files. It is recommended that you uninstall software which is not used on the computer as this can help to keep your system stable and speed it up. Do not remove any software that you are unsure of or do not recognise before carrying out intensive research as this could potentially damage the smooth running of your computer.

Upload(ing) – When someone sends a file or data from their computer to another computer. (See also 'Download'.)

URL (Uniform Resource Locator) – The Web address of a site on the internet. (See also 'Domain name'.)

USB – Introduced in the 1990s and typically in the form of a small cable, the USB (Universal Serial Bus) was developed to help standardise the connection of peripherals (such as printers, portable hard drives) to computers and has now superseded other connections such as the serial and parallel port.

Virus – A software program that is unknowingly installed onto your computer hard drive specifically to cause harm in some way (usually to obtain personal and/or private information or to cause physical damage to the system). Once a virus has managed to get into your computer it is extremely difficult to remove without anti-virus software. (See 'Anti-virus software'.)

Web (World Wide Web) – A system built on top of the internet which distributes information and data in the Hypertext Transfer Protocol (HTTP) language and uses a browser to display the information.

Web-based email – Rather than use a specific software program to send and receive emails such as Outlook, some websites offer a web-based email service where email correspondence is executed using browser software instead.

Website – The collection of webpages or documents/files that are linked together and available on the Web for visitors to find. Websites can be created by companies, organisations, associations and individuals.

Webmaster – The person responsible for creating, designing and administering/updating a website.

Worm – A small program that can reproduce and spread over a network. It has usually been created for malicious reasons and can have a very harmful effect on the infected systems.

WWW – The World Wide Web. (See also 'Web'.)

APPENDIX 2

Forms

COMPUTER INFORMATION FORM

Computer user: Name _____ User name _____

Email address(es) _____

Email password(s) _____

Machine/drive identifiers

Type (laptop, desktop, tablet) _____ Manufacturer _____

Model # _____ Serial # _____ Asset/inventory tag _____

Purchase details

Where was the machine purchased? _____

Attach a receipt to this document if you have one.

Date of purchase _____ Guarantee (years) _____

Operating software

Operating system is _____

Admin account or nickname _____

Admin operating system password _____

Computer specifications

Hard drive capacity _____ RAM _____ Graphics card capacity _____

Peripherals attached/removable to/near the specified system

Hard drives _____ CD-ROM Read-only _____

CD-ROM Read/write _____ Fax/modem _____

3.5 floppy _____ Printers _____

Zip/Jaz drive _____ USB ports _____

Docking station _____ Network connection _____

Floppies _____ Tapes _____

CD-ROMs _____ DVD-ROMs _____

Other not listed_____

Firewall/anti-virus software

Firewall information _____

Anti-virus information _____

Serial no. _____ Expiry date_____

Anti-spy/malware software _____

Serial no. _____ Expiry date_____

Other software installed

Name	Installation date	Serial number
_____	_____	_____
_____	_____	_____
_____	_____	_____
_____	_____	_____

Typical websites visited

Website name/address	Type of website	User name	Password
_____	_____	_____	_____
_____	_____	_____	_____
_____	_____	_____	_____
_____	_____	_____	_____

Notes _____

_____

★

CHILD'S COMPUTER ACTIVITY LOG

Date/time	Activity description	How I feel	Duration	Value (high, medium, low, none)
e.g. 19 June 1pm	Logged in to social network website	Happy	30 mins	Low

CHILD'S SOCIAL NETWORKING ACTIVITY LOG

Date/ time	Social network name	Website address/URL	User name	Password	Activity description	Child's emotion	Duration	Value (high, medium, low, none)
e.g. 19 June 1pm	Facebook	www.facebook.com	Neil123	Password	Logged in to chat to school mate Julie about homework	Happy	30 mins	High

MOBILE PHONE INFORMATION FORM

Telephone no. _____ PIN _____

Make _____ Model_____

Serial no. _____ IMEI no._____

Purchased from _____ Purchase date _____

Contract or pay as you go _____

Contract length (if applicable)_____

Estimated monthly cost_____

Features of phone

Internal memory _____ GB operating system _____

Memory card type _____ Processor _____

Other features: *Tick all that apply*

☐ Bluetooth   ☐ Conference calling

☐ Wireless tethering   ☐ Vibrating alert

☐ SatNav   ☐ Voice-activated dialling

☐ Wi-fi connection   ☐ Instant messaging

☐ GPS   ☐ Built-in speaker

☐ Camera/video   ☐ Call waiting/hold

☐ Games   ☐ Speed dialling

☐ App store   ☐ Video calling

☐ Music player   ☐ Internet and email

☐ Calendar   ☐ Web browser

☐ Microsoft Outlook   ☐ Alarm clock

☐ Picture/video messaging   ☐ Calendar

☐ Call divert/transfer   ☐ Stopwatch/timer

Parental controls

_____

_____

_____

CHILD'S COMPUTER LOG – HOURS PER WEEK

WEEK ENDING: _____

Time	Monday	Tuesday	Wednesday	Thursday	Friday	Saturday	Sunday	TOTAL
6am–8am								
8am–noon	e.g. 30 mins							30 mins
Noon–4pm								
4pm–8pm								
8pm–midnight	60 mins							60 mins
Midnight–6am								
TOTAL	90 mins							90 mins

★

CHILD'S COMPUTER LOG – COMPUTER TIME SLOT ALLOWANCE

WEEK ENDING: _____

Monday	Tuesday	Wednesday	Thursday	Friday	Saturday	Sunday
e.g. Made bed/tidied room						
Completed history homework						
30 mins						

SLOT = 15 mins

WORKSTATION SETTINGS FORM   ★

Lighting

Light to use (main light, desk lamp, etc.) _____

Min light-bulb wattage _____ Max light-bulb wattage: _____

Position of blinds (open/closed, etc.) _____

Position of curtains (open/closed, etc.) _____

Other _____

Room temperature

Min room temp _____ Max room temp _____

Ventilation (window open/air conditioning) _____

Other _____

Sound

Min speaker level setting _____ Max speaker level setting_____

Position of door (open/closed, etc.) _____

Position of window (open/closed, etc.) _____

Other _____

Chair setting

Chair height setting _____ Chair back position _____

Chair arm position setting _____

Other _____

Desk area

Mouse position setting _____

Keyboard settings _____

Other _____

References

CHILDWISE (2013–2014) *CHILDWISE Monitor Report 2013–14: Digital Lives.* Available at www.childwise.co.uk/childwise-published-research-detail.asp? PUBLISH=4, accessed on 9 September 2014.

Department for Education (2011) *The Protection of Children Online: A Brief Scoping Review to Identify Vulnerable Groups.* London: Department for Education. Available at www.gov.uk/government/publications/the-protection-of-children-online-a-brief-scoping-review-to-identify-vulnerable-groups, accessed on 13 May 2014.

Little, L. (2002) 'Middle-class mothers' perceptions of peer and sibling victimisation among children with Asperger's Syndrome and non-verbal learning disorders.' *Issues in Comprehensive Paediatric Nursing 25,* 1, 43–57.

Mazurek, M.O. and Engelhardt C.R. (2013) 'Video game use in boys with autism spectrum disorder, ADHD, or typical development.' *Pediatrics 132,* 260–266.

Ofcom (2013c) *Communications Market Report 2013.* London: Ofcom. Available at http://stakeholders.ofcom.org.uk/binaries/research/cmr/cmr13/2013_UK_CMR.pdf, accessed on 13 May 2014.

Ofcom (2013a) *Children and Parents: Media Use and Attitudes in the Nations, 2012 Metrics Bulletin.* London: Ofcom. Available at http://stakeholders.ofcom.org.uk/binaries/research/media-literacy/2012-Metrics-Bulletin/2012-Metrics-Bulletin.pdf, accessed on 13 May 2014.

Ofcom (2013b) *Children and Parents: Media Use and Attitudes Report.* London: Ofcom. Available at http://stakeholders.ofcom.org.uk/binaries/research/media-literacy/october-2013/research07Oct2013.pdf, accessed on 13 May 2014.

Olweus, D. (1993) 'Bully/victims problems among school-children: long-term consequences and an effective intervention program.' In S. Hodgins (ed.) *Mental Disorder and Crime.* Thousand Oaks, CA: Sage Publications, pp.317–349.

Sterzing, P.R., Shattuck, P.T., Narendorf, S.C., Wagner, M. and Cooper, B.P. (2012) 'Bullying involvement and Autism Spectrum Disorders: prevalence and correlates of bullying involvement among adolescents with an Autism Spectrum Disorder.' *Archives of Pediatric Adolescent Medicine 166,* 11, 1058–1064.

Texas State University Counseling Center. *Internet Addiction.* San Marcos, TX: Texas State University. Available at www.counseling.txstate.edu/resources/ shoverview/bro/interadd.html, accessed on 13 May 2014.

UK Council for Child Internet Safety (2012) *Good practice guidance for the providers of social networking and other user-interactive services.* London: Institute of Education, University of London. Available at http://dera.ioe.ac.uk/1970, accessed on 13 May 2014.

Wing, L. and Gould, J. (1979) 'Severe impairments of social interaction and associated abnormalities in children: epidemiology and classification.' *Journal of Autism and Childhood Schizophrenia 9,* 11–29.

Index